Afghanistan

Other Books of Related Interest:

Opposing Viewpoints Series
America's Global Influence

The Taliban

US Foreign Policy

At Issue Series
Does the World Hate the US?

Drones

Weapons of War

Women in Islam

Current Controversies Series
Islamophobia

The Middle East

Pakistan

US Government Corruption

"Congress shall make
no law . . . abridging
the freedom of speech,
or of the press."

First Amendment to the US Constitution

The basic foundation of our democracy is the First Amendment guarantee of freedom of expression. The Opposing Viewpoints series is dedicated to the concept of this basic freedom and the idea that it is more important to practice it than to enshrine it.

OPPOSING
VIEWPOINTS®
SERIES

Afghanistan

Noah Berlatsky, Book Editor

GREENHAVEN PRESS
A part of Gale, Cengage Learning

GALE
CENGAGE Learning·

Farmington Hills, Mich • San Francisco • New York • Waterville, Maine
Meriden, Conn • Mason, Ohio • Chicago

Elizabeth Des Chenes, *Director, Content Strategy*
Douglas Dentino, *Manager, New Product*

© 2015 Greenhaven Press, a part of Gale, Cengage Learning.

WCN: 01-100-101

Gale and Greenhaven Press are registered trademarks used herein under license.

For more information, contact:
Greenhaven Press
27500 Drake Rd.
Farmington Hills, MI 48331-3535
Or you can visit our Internet site at gale.cengage.com

For product information and technology assistance, contact us at

Gale Customer Support, 1-800-877-4253
For permission to use material from this text or product, submit all requests online at www.cengage.com/permissions

Further permissions questions can be emailed to permissionrequest@cengage.com

Articles in Greenhaven Press anthologies are often edited for length to meet page requirements. In addition, original titles of these works are changed to clearly present the main thesis and to explicitly indicate the author's opinion. Every effort is made to ensure that Greenhaven Press accurately reflects the original intent of the authors. Every effort has been made to trace the owners of copyrighted material.

Cover Image copyright © Nikolai Ignatiev/Alamy.

LIBRARY OF CONGRESS CATALOGING-IN-PUBLICATION DATA

Afghanistan / Noah Berlatsky, book editor.
    pages cm. -- -- (Opposing viewpoints)
    Includes bibliographical references and index.
    ISBN 978-0-7377-7242-5 (hardback) -- ISBN 978-0-7377-7243-2 (paperback)
    1. Postwar reconstruction--Afghanistan. 2. Nation-building--Afghanistan. 3. Internal security--Afghanistan. 4. Democratization--Afghanistan. 5. Human rights--Afghanistan. 6. United States--Foreign relations--Afghanistan. 7. Afghanistan--Foreign relations--United States. I. Berlatsky, Noah, editor of compilation.
    DS371.4.A328 2014
    958.104'7--dc23
                                                    2014021944

Contents

Why Consider Opposing Viewpoints?

> *"The only way in which a human being can make some approach to knowing the whole of a subject is by hearing what can be said about it by persons of every variety of opinion and studying all modes in which it can be looked at by every character of mind. No wise man ever acquired his wisdom in any mode but this."*
>
> *John Stuart Mill*

In our media-intensive culture it is not difficult to find differing opinions. Thousands of newspapers and magazines and dozens of radio and television talk shows resound with differing points of view. The difficulty lies in deciding which opinion to agree with and which "experts" seem the most credible. The more inundated we become with differing opinions and claims, the more essential it is to hone critical reading and thinking skills to evaluate these ideas. Opposing Viewpoints books address this problem directly by presenting stimulating debates that can be used to enhance and teach these skills. The varied opinions contained in each book examine many different aspects of a single issue. While examining these conveniently edited opposing views, readers can develop critical thinking skills such as the ability to compare and contrast authors' credibility, facts, argumentation styles, use of persuasive techniques, and other stylistic tools. In short, the Opposing Viewpoints Series is an ideal way to attain the higher-level thinking and reading skills so essential in a culture of diverse and contradictory opinions.

In addition to providing a tool for critical thinking, Opposing Viewpoints books challenge readers to question their own strongly held opinions and assumptions. Most people form their opinions on the basis of upbringing, peer pressure, and personal, cultural, or professional bias. By reading carefully balanced opposing views, readers must directly confront new ideas as well as the opinions of those with whom they disagree. This is not to argue simplistically that everyone who reads opposing views will—or should—change his or her opinion. Instead, the series enhances readers' understanding of their own views by encouraging confrontation with opposing ideas. Careful examination of others' views can lead to the readers' understanding of the logical inconsistencies in their own opinions, perspective on why they hold an opinion, and the consideration of the possibility that their opinion requires further evaluation.

Evaluating Other Opinions

To ensure that this type of examination occurs, Opposing Viewpoints books present all types of opinions. Prominent spokespeople on different sides of each issue as well as well-known professionals from many disciplines challenge the reader. An additional goal of the series is to provide a forum for other, less known, or even unpopular viewpoints. The opinion of an ordinary person who has had to make the decision to cut off life support from a terminally ill relative, for example, may be just as valuable and provide just as much insight as a medical ethicist's professional opinion. The editors have two additional purposes in including these less known views. One, the editors encourage readers to respect others' opinions—even when not enhanced by professional credibility. It is only by reading or listening to and objectively evaluating others' ideas that one can determine whether they are worthy of consideration. Two, the inclusion of such viewpoints encourages the important critical thinking skill of objectively evaluating an author's credentials and bias. This evaluation will illuminate an author's reasons for taking a particular stance on an issue and will aid in readers' evaluation of the author's ideas.

It is our hope that these books will give readers a deeper understanding of the issues debated and an appreciation of the complexity of even seemingly simple issues when good and honest people disagree. This awareness is particularly important in a democratic society such as ours in which people enter into public debate to determine the common good. Those with whom one disagrees should not be regarded as enemies but rather as people whose views deserve careful examination and may shed light on one's own.

Thomas Jefferson once said that "difference of opinion leads to inquiry, and inquiry to truth." Jefferson, a broadly educated man, argued that "if a nation expects to be ignorant and free . . . it expects what never was and never will be." As individuals and as a nation, it is imperative that we consider the opinions of others and examine them with skill and discernment. The Opposing Viewpoints series is intended to help readers achieve this goal.

David L. Bender and Bruno Leone,
Founders

Introduction

"Just 19% of likely U.S. voters believe it's
still possible for the United States to win
the war in Afghanistan, according to a
new Rasmussen Reports national tele-
phone survey. Fifty-four percent (54%)
don't think it's possible for the United
States to win the war. Twenty-seven percent (27%) are undecided."

—Rasmussen Reports,
"New Low: 19% Believe
U.S. Can Still Win War in
Afghanistan," October 15, 2013

The United States has stated that it plans to remove all or most of its troops from Afghanistan in 2014. That will conclude a thirteen-year American military involvement in Afghanistan—the longest war in American history. As the conflict ends, many are asking, did America win?

In general, the consensus is "no." In fact, some commenters have argued that the war has been lost for years. For example, Michael Scheuer, writing in the *Diplomat* argues as far back as July 1, 2010, that "the US-NATO coalition has lost a war its political leaders never meant, or knew how, to win." He goes on to say that by occupying the country, the United States had united Afghans against them and that American support for the illegitimate and corrupt President Hamid Karzai government had undermined any hope for victory. He adds that the United States failed to use the necessary overwhelming force and that the result has been "abject Western defeat."

More recent appraisals have echoed Scheuer's assessment. Thom Shanker, writing in a January 1, 2013, *New York Times* article, compares the American experience in Afghanistan to the failed Soviet occupation of the 1980s. "Despite the differences going in, both the Soviet Union and the United States soon learned that Afghanistan is a land where foreigners aspiring to create nations in their image must combat not just the Taliban but tribalism, orthodoxy, corruption and a medieval view of women," Shanker says. He adds that the United States should learn from the Soviet experience, which showed that Afghan forces fighting the Taliban could hold out without foreign forces, but only if supplied with sufficient aid. The Soviets, however, were ultimately defeated in Afghanistan, and Shanker's parallel suggests that the United States has been as well. That conclusion is underlined by a recent intelligence estimate that gains made by US and allied forces since 2011 "are likely to have been significantly eroded by 2017," even if several thousand US troops remain in Afghanistan, as reported by Ernesto Londoño, Karen DeYoung, and Greg Miller in a December 28, 2013, piece in the *Washington Post*.

Some commenters have argued, however, that the war in Afghanistan has not gone that badly and even that it remains winnable. For instance, Stewart Upton, in an October 24, 2012, article in *Foreign Policy*, argues that the media has failed to report on the significant military progress made in Afghanistan. He points out that in areas where the international forces have handed over activities to the Afghan National Security Forces (ANSF) "there has been no significant increase in either insurgent or criminal activity." That seems to bode well for future international withdrawal. "Don't underestimate ANSF's bravery or their willingness to put their lives on the line for their country," he says, "because they are doing it every single day."

In an April 4, 2012, article at the *Atlantic* by Micah Zenko, several commenters suggest that the United States may ultimately achieve at least some success in Afghanistan. Michael Wahid Hanna, a fellow at the Century Foundation, for example, argues that "the core goals of the Afghan war are still within reach for the Obama administration, as they are not reliant on the actual defeat of the Taliban." Rather, he says, the "core goals" are to weaken the terrorist group al Qaeda and deny it a strong footing in Afghanistan. Hanna argues that has been done. Further, he says that "the Taliban are also not in a position to topple the central government and reassert political control over all of Afghanistan." He admits that a stalemate with a continued American military presence of some sort in Afghanistan is not ideal, but he argues that there is still room to reach a negotiated solution with the Taliban.

Whether or not America won or will win the war, Afghanistan continues to present numerous challenges. The remainder of this book examines the most important of these in chapters titled "What Are Security Issues in Afghanistan?," "What Issues Confront Afghan Democracy?," "What Are Economic Issues in Afghanistan?" and "What Is the Human Rights Situation in Afghanistan?" Different viewpoints offer a range of possible ways for the international community to help Afghanistan deal with the many issues it faces.

**OPPOSING
VIEWPOINTS®
SERIES**

CHAPTER 1

What Are Security Issues in Afghanistan?

Chapter Preface

Kidnapping is a serious security issue in Afghanistan. The threat does not necessarily come from radical Islamic insurgents targeting Westerners or enemies in the name of the cause. Rather, kidnapping in Afghanistan is enabled by the lack of law and order, and "much of the threat is simply criminal," according to Matthieu Aikins, writing in an October 20, 2010, article on the *Foreign Policy* website. Foreigners, wealthy Afghans, and anyone who can likely pay is a target.

In fact, Aikins says, when coalition forces weaken the Taliban, the problem of kidnapping may actually worsen. As the Taliban has fragmented and key leaders have been killed, discipline and order in the insurgency have fractured. "The result is that guarantees of safe passage and years of connections with high-ranking Taliban are no longer a reliable way to safely travel through insurgent-controlled areas," Aikins writes. He adds that many kidnappers have ties with corrupt officials in the government and says some parliamentary candidates are known to be linked to kidnappers.

Aikins was writing in 2010, but the problem of kidnapping has continued. In an April 24, 2013, piece in the *Washington Post*, Kevin Sieff reports on a rash of kidnappings in the city of Herat. Herat is distant from the fight against the Taliban and is generally held up as a peaceable oasis in the Afghan conflict, with a growing economy and a progressive attitude toward women's rights. In 2012, however, five hundred people were arrested for kidnapping, an exponential increase from the twelve arrested five years earlier. Wealthy Afghans—including politicians, industrialists, and bankers—are targeted. "Other relatively peaceful parts of the country, including Kabul and Jalalabad" have also been affected, according to Sieff. The rash of kidnappings causes Sieff to ask, "What if eradicating the insurgency only creates space for a new generation of criminal networks?"

One terrible incident in Herat, reported by Sieff, involved the abduction and murder of a nine-year-old boy. In another incident, reported on January 21, 2014, by Reuters, sixty Afghans working for a British de-mining group were taken by gunmen en masse while working to clear land mines. Such kidnappings terrorize the local population and make it difficult to operate aid operations in the region.

The authors in the following chapter debate other security issues in Afghanistan related to American troop withdrawal and the relationship of other countries in the region to stabilizing the Afghan conflict.

> "Since outlasting the Taliban is unlikely,
> the only realistic alternative to even-
> tual defeat is a negotiated settlement."

The United States Needs to Reach a Negotiated Settlement with the Taliban

Stephen Biddle

Stephen Biddle is a historian, policy analyst, and columnist whose work concentrates on US foreign policy. He is the author of Military Power: Explaining Victory and Defeat in Modern Battle. *In the following viewpoint, he argues that the United States' only alternative to outright defeat in Afghanistan is a negotiated settlement with the Taliban. He says a settlement would allow the Taliban a good deal of power in Afghanistan, but it would at least keep the country from destabilizing the region or being a haven for terrorists against the United States. If the Barack Obama administration is not willing to negotiate for political reasons, he says, it should end the war immediately. Otherwise, slow disengagement will result in billions of dollars in wasted funds and an eventual Taliban victory.*

Stephen Biddle, "Ending the War in Afghanistan," *Foreign Affairs*, September–October 2013. Reprinted by permission of FOREIGN AFFAIRS, (issue 5/September/October 2013). Copyright © 2013 by the Council on Foreign Relations, Inc. www.ForeignAffairs.com.

As you read, consider the following questions:

1. What does Biddle estimate annual US military contribution to Afghanistan to be after US withdrawal, and how does that compare to US military aid to Israel?

2. What vital interests would America preserve in a negotiated settlement with the Taliban, according to Biddle?

3. What does Biddle predict will be the cost if the Obama administration continues with its current policy of slow disengagement?

International forces in Afghanistan are preparing to hand over responsibility for security to Afghan soldiers and police by the end of 2014. U.S. President Barack Obama has argued that battlefield successes since 2009 have enabled this transition and that with it, "this long war will come to a responsible end." But the war will not end in 2014. The U.S. role may end, in whole or in part, but the war will continue—and its ultimate outcome is very much in doubt.

Negotiation or Defeat

Should current trends continue, U.S. combat troops are likely to leave behind a grinding stalemate between the Afghan government and the Taliban [the militant Islamic force that once controlled Afghanistan]. The Afghan National Security Forces [ANSF] can probably sustain this deadlock, but only as long as the U.S. Congress pays the multibillion-dollar annual bills needed to keep them fighting. The war will thus become a contest in stamina between Congress and the Taliban. Unless Congress proves more patient than the Taliban leader Mullah [Mohammed] Omar, funding for the ANSF will eventually shrink until Afghan forces can no longer hold their ground, and at that point, the country could easily descend into chaos. If it does, the war will be lost and U.S. aims forfeited. A policy of simply handing off an ongoing war to an Afghan government that cannot afford the troops needed to win it is thus not a strategy for a "responsible end" to the conflict; it is closer to what the [Richard] Nixon administration was willing to accept in the final stages of the Vietnam War, a "decent interval" between the United States' withdrawal and the eventual defeat of its local ally.

There are only two real alternatives to this, neither of them pleasant. One is to get serious about negotiations with the Taliban. This is no panacea, but it is the only alternative to outright defeat. To its credit, the Obama administration has pursued such talks for over a year. What it has not done is spend the political capital needed for an actual deal. A settlement the United States could live with would require hard political engineering both in Kabul [the capital of Afghanistan] and on Capitol Hill, yet the administration has not followed through.

The other defensible approach is for the United States to cut its losses and get all the way out of Afghanistan now, leaving behind no advisory presence and reducing its aid substantially. Outright withdrawal might damage the United States' prestige, but so would a slow-motion version of the same defeat—only at a greater cost in blood and treasure. And although a speedy U.S. withdrawal would cost many Afghans their lives and freedoms, fighting on simply to postpone such consequences temporarily would needlessly sacrifice more American lives in a lost cause.

The Obama administration has avoided both of these courses, choosing instead to muddle through without incurring the risk and political cost that a sustainable settlement would require. Time is running out, however, and the administration should pick its poison. Paying the price for a real settlement is a better approach than quick withdrawal, but both are better than halfhearted delay. For the United States, losing per se is not the worst-case scenario; losing expensively is. Yet that is exactly what a myopic focus on a short-term transition without the political work needed to settle the war will probably produce: failure on the installment plan.

The Coming Stalemate

The international coalition fighting in Afghanistan has long planned on handing over responsibility for security there to local Afghan forces. But the original idea was that before doing so, a troop surge would clear the Taliban from strategically critical terrain and weaken the insurgency so much that the war would be close to a finish by the time the Afghans took over. That never happened. The surge made important progress, but the tight deadlines for a U.S. withdrawal and the Taliban's resilience have left insurgents in control of enough territory to remain militarily viable well after 2014. Afghan government forces will thus inherit a more demanding job than expected.

The forces [who are] supposed to carry out this job are a mixed lot. The ANSF's best units should be capable of modest offensive actions to clear Taliban strongholds; other units' corruption and ineptitude will leave them part of the problem rather than part of the solution for the foreseeable future. On balance, it is reasonable to expect that the ANSF will be able to hold most or all of the terrain the surge cleared but not expand the government's control much beyond that. Although the Taliban will probably not march into Kabul after coalition combat troops leave, the war will likely be deadlocked, grinding onward as long as someone pays the bills to keep the ANSF operating.

Those bills will be substantial, and Congress will have to foot most of them. The coalition has always understood that an ANSF powerful enough to hold what the surge gained would be vastly more expensive than what the Afghan government could afford. In fiscal year 2013, the ANSF's operating budget of $6.5 billion was more than twice as large as the Afghan government's entire federal revenue. Most of the money to keep the ANSF fighting will thus have to come from abroad, and the lion's share from the United States.

In principle, this funding should look like a bargain. According to most estimates, after the transition, the United States will contribute some $4–$6 billion annually to the ANSF—a pittance compared to the nearly $120 billion it spent in 2011 to wage the war with mostly American troops. The further one gets from 2011, however, the less salient that contrast becomes and the more other comparisons will come to mind. Annual U.S. military aid to Israel, for example, totaled $3.1 billion in fiscal year 2013; the amount required to support the ANSF will surely exceed this for a long time. And unlike Israel, which enjoys powerful political support in Washington, there is no natural constituency for Afghan military aid in American politics.

Afghan aid will get even harder to defend the next time an Afghan corruption scandal hits the newspapers, or Afghan protests erupt over an accidental Koran burning, or an American adviser is killed by an Afghan recipient of U.S. aid, or an Afghan president plays to local politics by insulting American sensibilities. Such periodic crises are all but inevitable, and each one will sap congressional support for aid to Afghanistan. I recently spoke to a gathering of almost 70 senior congressional staffers with an interest in Afghanistan and asked how many of them thought it was likely that the ANSF aid budget would be untouched after one of these crises. None did.

In the near term, Congress will probably pay the ANSF what the White House requests, but the more time goes on, the more likely it will be that these appropriations will be cut back. It will not take much reduction in funds before the ANSF contracts to a size that is smaller than what it needs to be to hold the line or before a shrinking pool of patronage money splits the institution along factional lines. Either result risks a return to the civil warfare of the 1990s, which would provide exactly the kind of militant safe haven that the United States has fought since 2001 to prevent.

Managing the congressional politics around sustaining Afghan forces after the transition was feasible back when Washington assumed that a troop surge before the transition would put the Taliban on a glide path to extinction. The United States would still have had to give billions of dollars a year to the ANSF, but the war would have ended relatively quickly. After that, it would have been possible to demobilize large parts of the ANSF and turn the remainder into a peacetime establishment; aid would then have shrunk to lower levels, making congressional funding a much easier sell. But that is not the scenario that will present itself in 2014. With an indefinite stalemate on the horizon instead, the politics of funding the ANSF will be much harder to handle—and without a settlement, that funding will outlast the Taliban's will to fight only if one assumes heroic patience on the part of Congress.

Let's Make a Deal

Since outlasting the Taliban is unlikely, the only realistic alternative to eventual defeat is a negotiated settlement. The administration has pursued such a deal for well over a year, but so far the process has yielded little, and there is now widespread skepticism about the talks.

Many, for example, doubt the Taliban are serious about the negotiations. After all, in late 2011, they assassinated Burhanuddin Rabbani, the head of Afghan president Hamid Karzai's High Peace Council and the Kabul official charged with moving the talks forward. Since the Taliban can wait out the United States and win outright, why should they make concessions? Others argue that the Taliban are interested in negotiations only insofar as they provide a source of legitimacy and a soapbox for political grandstanding. Still others worry that bringing together multiple Taliban factions, their

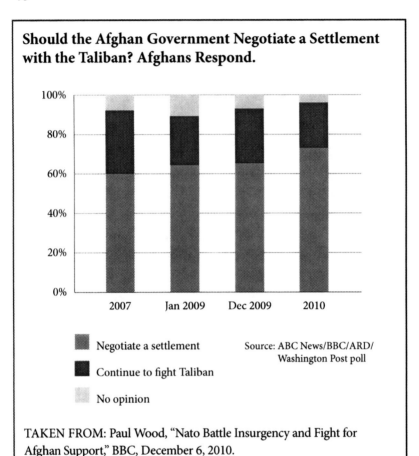

Should the Afghan Government Negotiate a Settlement with the Taliban? Afghans Respond.

Negotiate a settlement

Continue to fight Taliban

No opinion

Source: ABC News/BBC/ARD/
Washington Post poll

TAKEN FROM: Paul Wood, "Nato Battle Insurgency and Fight for Afghan Support," BBC, December 6, 2010.

Pakistani patrons, the Karzai administration, the governments of the United States and its allies, and intermediaries such as Qatar will simply prove too complex. Conservatives in the United States, meanwhile, doubt the Obama administration's motives, worrying that negotiating with the enemy signals weakness and fearing that the White House will make unnecessary concessions simply to cover its rush to the exits. Liberals fear losing hard-won gains for Afghan women and minorities. And many Afghans, especially women's groups and those who are not part of the country's Pashtun majority, also worry about that outcome, and some have even threatened civil war to prevent it.

Yet despite these concerns, there is still a chance for a deal that offers more than just a fig leaf to conceal policy failure. The Taliban have, after all, publicly declared that they are willing to negotiate—a costly posture, since the Taliban are not a monolithic actor but an alliance of factions. When Mullah Omar's representatives accept talks, other factions worry about deals being made behind their backs. Taliban field commanders wonder whether the battlefield prognosis is as favorable as their leaders claim (if victory is near, why negotiate?) and face the challenge of motivating fighters to risk their lives when shadowy negotiations might render such sacrifice unnecessary. The Taliban's willingness to accept these costs thus implies some possible interest in a settlement.

Why the Taliban Negotiate

There may be good reasons for the Taliban to explore a deal. Mullah Omar and his allies in the leadership have been living in exile in Pakistan for over a decade—their children are growing up as Pakistanis—and their movements are surely constrained by their Pakistani patrons. Afghans are famously nationalist, and the Afghan-Pakistani rivalry runs deep; exile across the border surely grates on the Afghan Taliban. Perhaps more important, they live under the constant threat of assassination by U.S. drones or commando raids: just ask Osama bin Laden or six of the last seven al Qaeda operations directors, all killed or captured in such attacks. And a stalemate wastes the lives and resources of the Taliban just as it does those of the Afghan forces and their allies. While the Taliban are probably able to pay this price indefinitely, and while they will surely not surrender just to stanch the bleeding, this does not mean they would prefer continued bloodletting to any possible settlement. The conflict is costly enough that the Taliban might consider an offer if it is not tantamount to capitulation.

What would such a deal comprise? In principle, a bargain could be reached that preserved all parties' vital interests even if no one's ideal aims were achieved. The Taliban would have to renounce violence, break with al Qaeda, disarm, and accept something along the lines of today's Afghan constitution. In exchange, they would receive legal status as a political party, set-asides of offices or parliamentary seats, and the withdrawal of any remaining foreign forces from Afghanistan. The Afghan government, meanwhile, would have to accept a role for the Taliban in a coalition government and the springboard for Taliban political activism that this would provide. In exchange, the government would be allowed to preserve the basic blue-print of today's state, and it would surely command the votes needed to lead a governing coalition, at least in the near term. Pakistan would have to give up its blue-sky ambitions for an Afghan puppet state under Taliban domination, but it would gain a stable border and enough influence via its Taliban proxies to prevent any Afghan-Indian axis that could threaten it. And the United States, for its part, would have to accept the Taliban as a legal political actor, with an extra-democratic guarantee of positions and influence, and the probable forfei-ture of any significant base structure for conducting counter-terrorist operations from Afghan soil.

From Washington's perspective, this outcome would be far from ideal. It would sacrifice aims the United States has sought since 2001, putting at risk the hard-won rights of Afghan women and minorities by granting the Taliban a voice in Af-ghan politics and offering a share of power to an organization with the blood of thousands of Americans on its hands. Yet if properly negotiated, such a deal could at least preserve the two most vital U.S. national interests at stake in Afghanistan: that Afghanistan not become a base for militants to attack the West and that it not become a base for destabilizing the country's neighbors.

As long as the Taliban are denied control of internal secu-rity ministries or district or provincial governments in critical border areas, the non-Taliban majority in a coalition government could ensure that Afghanistan not become a home to terrorist camps like those that existed before the war. Chaos without a meaningful central government, by contrast, would preclude nothing. And whatever fate Afghan women and minorities suffered under a stable coalition would be far less bad than what they would face under anarchy. A compromise with the Taliban would be a bitter pill to swallow, but at this point, it would sacrifice less than the alternatives.

Getting to Yes

Simply meeting with the Taliban is only the starting point of the negotiating process. To create a deal that can last, the U.S. government and its allies will need to go far beyond this, starting by laying the political groundwork in Afghanistan. Although negotiators will not have an easy time getting anti-Taliban northerners to accept concessions, the biggest hurdle is predatory misgovernance in Kabul. Any settlement will have to legalize the Taliban and grant them a political foothold. This foothold would not give them control of the government, but their legal status would allow them to compete electorally and expand their position later. Over the longer term, therefore, the containment of the Taliban's influence will depend on political competition from a credible and attractive alternative—something the establishment in Kabul is not yet able or willing to provide.

The Taliban are not popular in Afghanistan; that is why they will accept a deal only if it guarantees them a certain level of representation in the government. But at least they are seen as incorruptible, whereas Karzai's government is deeply corrupt, exclusionary, and getting worse. If Karzai's successor continues this trend, he will hand the Taliban their best opportunity for real power. Should Kabul's misgovernance persist and worsen, eventually even a brutal but honest opposition movement will make headway. And if a legalized Taliban were to eventually control critical border districts, enabling their militant Pakistani allies to cash in some wartime IOUs and establish base camps under the Taliban's protection, the result could be nearly as dangerous to the West as the Afghan government's military defeat. The only real insurance against that outcome is for Kabul to change its ways.

To date, however, the West has been unwilling to compel reform, preferring so-called capacity-building aid to coercive diplomacy. Such benign assistance might be enough if the problem were merely a lack of capacity. But Afghanistan is misgoverned because its power brokers profit from such malfeasance; they won't change simply because the Americans ask them to, and unconditional capacity building just creates better-trained kleptocrats. Real improvement would require, among other things, that donors withhold their assistance if the Afghan government fails to implement reforms. But donors have shied away from true conditionality for fear that their bluff will be called, aid will have to be withheld, and the result will be a delay in the creation of a higher-capacity Afghan civil and military administration—the key to current plans for Western military withdrawal.

Politics, at Home and Abroad

If the West cannot credibly threaten to withhold something Kabul values, then Afghan governance will never improve. It is late in the game to begin such an approach now; the West would have had more leverage back when its aid budgets were larger and military resources more plentiful. Still, credible conditionality could make even a smaller budget into a stronger tool for reform. Using conditionality properly, however, would mean accepting the possibility that the West might have to deliberately reduce the capacity of Afghan institutions if they refuse to reform—a task that is neither easy nor pleasant, but necessary if the West is going to be serious about a settlement.

The Obama administration will need to undertake serious political work in Washington as well as in Kabul. Any viable settlement will take years to negotiate and require the West to make real concessions, and such a process will offer ample opportunities for members of Congress to embrace demagoguery and act as spoilers. The Obama administration's initial experience on this score is instructive: as an early confidence-building gesture, last year [2012] the administration offered to free five Taliban detainees at Guantánamo in exchange for the release of Sergeant Bowe Bergdahl, the Taliban's only American prisoner. But U.S. lawmakers howled in outrage, the detainees were not released, the Taliban charged bad faith (both on the detainee issue and on the addition of new conditions from Karzai), and the negotiations collapsed. [Editor's note: Bergdahl was released on May 31, 2014, as part of a prisoner exchange for five Taliban members who were being held at the detention center at Guantánamo Bay.] Serious negotiations toward a final peace settlement would provide countless opportunities for such congressional outrage, over much larger issues, and if legislators play such games—and if the administration lets itself be bullied—then a viable settlement will be impossible. Likewise, if Congress defunds the war too soon, unfinished negotiations will collapse as the Taliban seize victory on the battlefield with no need for concessions.

For talks to succeed, Congress will thus need to engage in two acts of selfless statesmanship: accepting concessions to the Taliban and prolonging unpopular aid to the Afghan military. The latter, in particular, would require bipartisan compromise, and achieving either or both goals may prove impossible. If they are going to happen, however, one prerequisite will be a sustained White House effort aimed at building the congressional support needed. The president will have to make a major investment in garnering political backing for a controversial Afghan policy, something he has not done so far.

Fish or Cut Bait

As daunting as the obstacles to a negotiated settlement are, such a deal still represents the least bad option for the United States in Afghanistan. If the White House is unwilling to accept the costs that a serious settlement effort would entail, however, then it is time to cut American losses and get out of Afghanistan now.

Some might see the Obama administration's current policy as a hedged version of such disengagement already. The U.S. military presence in Afghanistan will soon shrink to perhaps 8,000–12,000 advisers and trainers, and U.S. aid might decline to $4–$5 billion a year for the ANSF and $2–$3 billion in economic assistance, with the advisory presence costing perhaps another $8–$12 billion a year. This commitment is far smaller than the 100,000 U.S. troops and over $100 billion of 2011, and it offers some chance of muddling through to an acceptable outcome while discreetly concealing the United States' probable eventual failure behind a veil of continuing modest effort.

Only in Washington, however, could $14–$20 billion a year be considered cheap. If this yielded a stable Afghanistan, it would indeed be a bargain, but if, as is likely without a settlement, it produces only a defeat drawn out over several years, it will mean needlessly wasting tens of billions of dollars. In a fiscal environment in which $8 billion a year for the Head Start preschool program or $36 billion a year for Pell Grant scholarships is controversial, it is hard to justify spending another $70–$100 billion in Afghanistan over, say, another half decade of stalemated warfare merely to disguise failure or defer its political consequences.

It is harder still to ask Americans to die for such a cause. Even an advisory mission involves risk, and right now, thousands of U.S. soldiers are continuing to patrol the country. If failure is coming, many Afghans will inevitably die, but a faster withdrawal could at least save some American lives that would be sacrificed along the slower route.

It would be preferable for the war to end a different way: through a negotiated compromise with the Taliban. Talks so complicated and fraught, of course, might fail even if the United States does everything possible to facilitate them. But without such efforts, the chances of success are minimal, and the result is likely to be just a slower, more expensive version of failure. Getting out now is a better policy than that.

"Think of the Taliban as a high schooler intent on flirting with you, and absolutely opposed to dating you. At a certain point, it becomes humiliating to keep asking for a night out to dinner and a movie."

Talks with the Taliban: First Failure, Then Humiliation

Isaac Chotiner

Isaac Chotiner is a senior editor at the New Republic. *In the following viewpoint, he argues that the Taliban in Afghanistan has shown no interest in serious negotiations and that pursuing the group in an effort to negotiate is futile and humiliating. He says that Hamid Karzai's efforts to negotiate with the Taliban behind the backs of Americans went nowhere and ended up sowing distrust among the anti-Taliban forces. Meanwhile, Chotiner argues, Pakistan's efforts to negotiate with the Taliban in that country have not even managed to slow terrorist attacks and simply emphasize that Pakistan does not control its own territory. Chotiner concludes that efforts to negotiate with the Taliban should cease.*

As you read, consider the following questions:

1. What examples of Karzai's erratic behavior does the *New York Times* discuss?

2. What does Chotiner say are some of the numerous problems with Pakistan's negotiating with the Taliban?

3. What are the real things tearing apart Pakistani society, according to Chotiner?

Since it became apparent several years ago that both the Afghan and Pakistani states were either unable or unwilling to wage full-on war against the Taliban groups that plague both countries, the word on every diplomat's list has been "talks." Sitting down with the Taliban, the theory went, was the only way to end the war in Afghanistan and bring peace to the country's eastern neighbor, Pakistan. The Taliban may be a band of murderous thugs, but you should not refuse to talk to people simply because they are evil. Force wasn't working; this was the only remaining option. And Taliban spokesmen claimed that the groups they represented were ready for dialogue. (Update: The *Washington Post* is now reporting that the United States is limiting drone strikes in Pakistan while the country pursues negotiations.)

Well, it is now 2014, and the United States is set to pull the vast majority—and perhaps all—of its forces from Afghanistan. And where are we with the much vaunted talks? Nowhere.

The failure is not proof that force is the answer to every problem, or that negotiating with unsavory people is by definition a mistake. But the push for talks with these particular unsavory people has now surpassed the point of no return and reached the point of deep embarrassment and humiliation. Diplomats and statesmen continue to push hard for talks ... and the Taliban simply refuses to negotiate in good faith, or with the intent to make peace. Think of the Taliban as a high schooler intent on flirting with you, and absolutely opposed to dating you. At a certain point, it becomes humiliating to keep asking for a night out to dinner and a movie.

First to Afghanistan: The *New York Times*'s blockbuster story on Tuesday, which revealed Hamid Karzai's secret negotiations with the Taliban, has been met with much hand-wringing and anger. The Afghan president, who has been unwilling to sign a long-term security agreement with the Americans, has actually been going behind the American government's back and attempting to woo the Taliban. The report of these secret contacts at least go some way to explaining Karzai's rather bizarre and erratic behavior. As the *Times* states:

> The secret contacts appear to help explain a string of actions by Mr. Karzai that seem intended to antagonize his American backers, Western and Afghan officials said. In recent weeks, Mr. Karzai has continued to refuse to sign a long-term security agreement with Washington that he negotiated, insisted on releasing hardened Taliban militants from prison and distributed distorted evidence of what he called American war crimes.

These actions have enraged American officials, as has the idea that Karzai would reach out to groups that are killing Afghans and American soldiers. But what's truly embarrassing and maddening about Karzai's unilateral initiative is that it is, er, absolutely pointless. As the *Times* reports: "The clandestine contacts with the Taliban have borne little fruit, according to people who have been told about them. But they have helped undermine the remaining confidence between the United States and Mr. Karzai, making the already messy endgame of the Afghan conflict even more volatile." Even worse:

> The peace contacts, though, have yielded no tangible agreement, nor even progressed as far as opening negotiations for one. And it is not clear whether the Taliban ever intended to

seriously pursue negotiations, or were simply trying to de-rail the security agreement by distracting Mr. Karzai and leading him on, as many of the officials said they suspected.

Karzai's move was not just nefarious; it was dumb. As the *Times* notes:

Why would the insurgency agree to talks if doing so would ensure the presence of the foreign troops it is determined to expel?

A good question—and one that those who want to talk might mull over.

Across the "border" in Pakistan, things look equally bleak. The incumbent government, headed by Prime Minister Nawaz Sharif, is all set to embark on talks with the Pakistani Taliban (TTP), which to date has killed tens of thousands of Pakistani citizens. The problems with such an approach are numerous: The Taliban does not accept Pakistan's government as legiti-mate; the Talibs have shown no willingness to curb terrorist attacks against military and civilian targets; and any compro-mise with such groups would presumably undermine the foundations of the Pakistani state, which should be able to ex-ert control over its territory, and which should not need to negotiate with a bunch of murderers who have a nebulous and sinister agenda. (Imagine the United States government negotiating with a collection of fascist nut bags over who gets to control a chunk of western Idaho. The very thought of it is embarrassing.)

The push for peace talks in Pakistan is being led by the opposition leader and former cricket star Imran Khan, who seems to think that Pakistan was more peaceful than Sweden before drone attacks, and who thinks the Taliban are a conse-quence, rather than a cause, of the war on terrorism. There is almost nothing that Imran does not blame on drones and un-named outsiders, including attacks on minority Shia Muslims, or just general Taliban violence. If there is any irony deriving

Taliban Terror in Pakistan

While Pakistan may consider India its greatest external foe, within the nation's borders the largest threat is perhaps the Taliban. By the summer of 2009, the Taliban had been behind a series of terrorist attacks that killed several thousands of Pakistanis, and efforts by the Pakistani government to reach peace deals with the Taliban have been unsuccessful. However, Pakistan did receive good news in August 2009 when the country's Taliban leader, Baitullah Mehsud, was killed by a U.S. Predator drone air strike.

According to an article published in the magazine *Foreign Policy*, a month before his death, Mehsud had led a corps of 16,000 fighters, both domestic and international, for five years. During that time, Mehsud was behind such acts as suicide bombings, taking three hundred Pakistani soldiers hostage (they were later exchanged for twenty-five imprisoned Taliban), and reportedly the assassination of former prime minister Benazir Bhutto. Mehsud had also threatened to attack Washington, D.C. Although his death prevented his threat from coming true, Mehsud and his Taliban operation were said to be responsible for 90 percent of the terrorist attacks in Pakistan, so his death should strike a serious blow for the Taliban's operations in the nation.

However, given the network of terrorists that Mehsud was able to train during his years of leadership, it may be naïve to think that the Taliban will not continue to be a threat both inside and outside Pakistan.

Laura Egendorf, ed.
"How Can Pakistan Address Terrorism?"
Pakistan. *Detroit: Greenhaven Press, 2010.*

from the fact that the violence is actually being done by entities—the Taliban, its terrorist allies—that right-wing Pakistanis and their military masters have done so much to nur-
ture and arm, and that which now seem so enamored of Khan
himself, it is lost (as is so much else) on the former playboy.

Thus, in the context of Pakistani politics, blathering on
and on about talks is actually a way of shirking the real things
that are tearing apart Pakistani society: ethnic violence, religious extremism, and intolerance. But rather than take these
forces on in a direct way, politicians continue to push talks.
Babar Sattar, one of the country's best columnists, has an ex-
cellent rundown of all the instances in which "deals" with ex-
tremists have broken down, thanks to their unwillingness to
actually follow through. But Sharif and his government keep
pathetically begging for sit-downs with an entity that remains
intent on killing Pakistanis without care or remorse. (Tuesday's
big suicide attack was in Peshawar; nine dead, fifty injured.)

(An even more cynical take on the strategy of the Pakistani government would be this: Most of the people dying live
outside of Punjab, the province of the country that houses the
business, political, and military elite. As long as their wealth
and safety isn't threatened, then so what if some people from
Balochistan or Sindh or Peshawar die every day? Why rock an
already unstable boat? This may be shortsighted—especially if
the Taliban and its allies keep gaining strength—but it makes
short-term sense.)

Is there anything that the Taliban and its allies can do to
make the leaders of either country believe that it is not interested in talks or negotiation? Is there anything that can put an
end to this pathetic spectacle? Commentators are prone to
overstating things like "honor" and "toughness" but it can't be
good for the people of either Pakistan or Afghanistan to see
their leaders bowing down before groups that would enslave
and kill them and their constituents. 2014 is going to be a
long year.

> "So the United States should . . . simply walk away with its troops and cash, thus cutting its losses and ending a quagmire that was lost long ago."

The United States Should Completely Withdraw Forces from Afghanistan

Ivan Eland

Ivan Eland is an author and a defense analyst, as well as a senior fellow and director of the Center on Peace and Liberty at the Independent Institute. In the following viewpoint, he argues that the United States will gain little by leaving a residual force in Afghanistan. He says that the Taliban knows that the United States is going to withdraw, and with reduced US forces, it will make gains against the government in Kabul. America has few real security interests in what is essentially a civil war. Eland concludes that the United States should withdraw completely from Afghanistan as soon as possible.

As you read, consider the following questions:

1. What is the sticking point preventing an agreement on a US residual force in Afghanistan, according to Eland?

Ivan Eland, "As in Iraq, Completely Withdraw US Forces from Afghanistan," AntiWar .com, October 23, 2013. Copyright © 2013 by Ivan Eland. Reproduced by permission.

2. What does Eland say the British learned in Yemen in the 1960s?

3. How many terrorists does Eland suggest are in Afghanistan, and what effect does he say this should have on US policy?

Recently, Afghan President Hamid Karzai and U.S. Secretary of State John Kerry announced that they had agreed on key provisions of a security arrangement that could allow some American forces in Afghanistan to remain after the NATO [North Atlantic Treaty Organization] combat mission ends at the end of 2014. Yet no details were released on the deal, and remaining US troops' immunity from the indigenous justice system—which also led to the scuttling of a significant residual presence of American forces in Iraq—appears to be the sticking point. Earlier this issue had seemed to be resolved and the remaining issues were Afghan demands that the United States pledge to defend Afghanistan as it would a NATO ally and an Afghan desire to prohibit US special operations forces from continuing raids on Afghan villages.

An Unwinnable War

The demand of the United States to try any misbehavior of American troops in the US, rather than the Afghan, justice system is a rather imperial one, but apparently nonnegotiable with the Americans—at least if the outcome in Iraq is any indication. Although it is unclear how the other two issues were resolved (or whether they really are), the United States signing up to defend yet another country—especially one as destitute and incapable of providing it any help as Afghanistan—would be a continuing monetary sinkhole in a time of staggering US debt. Even more important, it might eventually involve heavier US attacks into Pakistan, a nominal US ally that is providing support for the US and Afghan enemy—the Afghan Taliban. Finally, if US special operation raids on the few suspected al

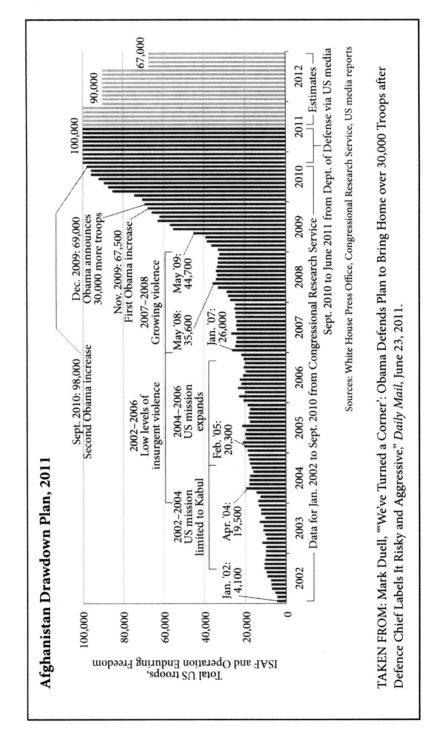

Afghanistan Drawdown Plan, 2011

TAKEN FROM: Mark Duell, "'We've Turned a Corner': Obama Defends Plan to Bring Home over 30,000 Troops after Defence Chief Labels It Risky and Aggressive," *Daily Mail*, June 23, 2011.

Qaeda [an Islamic terrorist organization] targets remaining in Afghanistan were prohibited, the only remotely justifiable reason for leaving American troops in the country would be gone. (The other remaining mission of training Afghan security forces provides little benefit to US security.)

Long ago, US commanders had said the Afghan war was unwinnable on the battlefield and that a negotiated settlement was required. The problem is, because of plummeting support for the war at home, President Barack Obama pledged to withdraw US forces by the end of 2014. As the British learned in Yemen during the 1960s, when the occupying power announces when it is exiting, guerrillas just stay in the field and wait for the stronger party's departure. In other words, the Taliban has no incentive to negotiate for lesser results when they can get most of what they want just by waiting. Also, many Afghans, knowing that the Taliban will remain long after US forces withdraw, will begin cooperating with the insurgents even though some may not want to.

Obama's dilemma shows that guerrilla wars are difficult for democracies to win, because they are often protracted and the key center of gravity is at home rather than in the occupied country (the same was true in the Vietnam War). One lesson is that if you are in one, don't announce when you are leaving even if you are. The more important lesson is to be very wary of getting into such brushfire wars in the first place, because they are likely bogs.

Cut the Losses

According to US intelligence, al Qaeda in Afghanistan/Pakistan is no longer even the biggest al Qaeda threat to the United States. Keeping troops in Afghanistan to battle roughly 50 suspected terrorists is needless. The real reason that the United States wants to retain some forces in Afghanistan is to protect the capital and keep the Taliban from taking that symbolic location. Many Afghans fear that upon US withdrawal, the Kabul government could disintegrate and civil war could resume. In fact, the few thousand US troops that would remain under any deal likely would be in the middle of a more intense civil war than what already has occurred for the last 13 years. The necessity of their mission for US security is highly questionable and their protection would be problematical.

Lastly, proponents of retaining US forces say that if all US forces are removed from Afghanistan, Congress will be far less likely to keep providing the $4 to $6 billion per year needed to prop the rickety Afghan security forces, which have already proven a sinkhole for $40 billion in wasted US aid. (In Vietnam War, Congress cut off US aid to the South Vietnamese government after US forces withdrew.) Yet saving this ineffectual expenditure would not be a bad outcome.

US commanders have maintained that Afghan forces have held their own against the Taliban, even though they took heavy casualties. But in guerrilla warfare, if the insurgents are not losing they are winning by just keeping an army in the field, and the rebels will likely do much better when the Americans leave, even according to US government officials.

So the United States should use any Afghan claims of sovereignty in the negotiation over any remaining US military presence to simply walk away with its troops and cash, thus cutting its losses and ending a quagmire that was lost long ago.

> "U.S. officials should not allow a troop drawdown to turn into a rush for the exits that would lead to greater instability in Afghanistan."

The United States Should Retain Troops in Afghanistan

Lisa Curtis

Lisa Curtis is a senior research fellow for South Asia in the Asian Studies Center at the Heritage Foundation. In the following viewpoint, she argues that the United States needs to retain a troop presence in Afghanistan to ensure that the Taliban does not take over and to prevent the terrorist group al Qaeda from reestablishing a presence in the country. She adds that talks with the Taliban are fruitless, since the group will not negotiate in good faith. She also says that the Barack Obama administration has consistently fumbled Afghan policy.

As you read, consider the following questions:

1. According to Curtis, how did the Obama administration blunder in its handling of the opening of the Taliban political office in Doha?

Lisa Curtis, "Afghanistan: Zero Troops Should Not Be an Option," Heritage Foundation, Issue Brief, no. 3986, July 10, 2013. Copyright © 2013 by The Heritage Foundation. All rights reserved. Reproduced by permission.

2. How many troops does Curtis say US and coalition forces should keep in Afghanistan after 2014?

3. What is the Haqqani network?

The [Barack] Obama administration is considering leaving no U.S. troops behind in Afghanistan after it ends its combat mission there in 2014. This would undermine U.S. security interests, as it would pave the way for the Taliban [militant Islamic group] to regain influence in Afghanistan and cripple the U.S. ability to conduct counterterrorism missions in the region.

President Obama instead should commit the U.S. to maintaining a robust troop presence (at least 15,000–20,000) in Afghanistan after 2014 in order to train and advise the Afghan troops and conduct counterterrorism missions as necessary. The U.S. should also remain diplomatically, politically, and financially engaged in Afghanistan in order to sustain the gains made over the past decade and ensure that the country does not again serve as a sanctuary for international terrorists intent on attacking the U.S.

Flaring Tensions Fuel Poor Policy Decisions

Tensions between the Obama and [Afghan president Hamid] Karzai administrations have escalated in recent months. The U.S. administration blundered in its handling of the opening of a Taliban political office in Doha in mid-June. In sending a U.S. delegation to Doha to meet with the Taliban leadership without the presence of the Afghan government, the Taliban appeared to be achieving its long-sought objective of cutting the Karzai administration out of the talks.

The Taliban also scored a public relations coup by raising the flag associated with its five-year oppressive rule in front of the office. The episode angered Afghan president Hamid Karzai to the point that he pulled out of the bilateral security agreement (BSA) talks with the U.S., thus fulfilling another Taliban goal of driving a wedge between the U.S. and Afghan governments.

Karzai's opposition to the U.S. talking unilaterally with the Taliban is understandable, but his decision to pull out of the BSA talks is misguided, since maintaining an international troop presence post-2014 is essential to the stability of the Afghan state and the ability of Afghan forces to protect against the use of its territory for international terrorism. The BSA talks are necessary to forge an agreement on a post-2014 U.S. troop presence.

If the White House is publicizing its consideration of the zero-troop option to try to pressure the Karzai administration, it also is misguided in its negotiating tactics. The Afghans already believe the U.S. is likely to cut and run, similar to the way Washington turned its back on the Afghans over two decades ago when the Soviets conceded defeat and pulled out of the country.

The Obama administration's failure to reach agreement with the Iraqi government on the terms for a residual U.S. force presence there highlights the White House's poor track record in managing these kinds of negotiations.

The Taliban leadership has shown no sign that it is ready to compromise for peace in Afghanistan. The Taliban has refused to talk directly with the Karzai government, calling it a puppet of the U.S., and has shown little interest in participating in a normal political process. The Taliban appears to believe that it is winning the war in Afghanistan and simply needs to wait out U.S. and NATO [North Atlantic Treaty Organization] forces. The insurgent leaders' only motivation for engaging with U.S. officials appears to be to obtain prisoner releases and to encourage the U.S. to speed up its troop withdrawals. The Taliban has already scored tactical points through the dialogue process by playing the U.S. and Afghans off one another and establishing international legitimacy with other governments.

Moreover, the Taliban has not tamped down violence in order to prepare an environment conducive to talks. In fact, in recent weeks Taliban insurgents have stepped up attacks. In early June [2013], for instance, insurgents conducted a suicide attack near the international airport in Kabul, and two weeks later they attacked the Afghan presidential palace.

Perseverance Required to Achieve U.S. Objectives

As difficult as the job may be, it is essential that the U.S. remain engaged in Afghanistan. It would be shortsighted to ignore the likely perilous consequences of the U.S. turning its back on this pivotal country from where the 9/11 attacks [referring to the September 11, 2001, attacks on the United States] originated. Moving forward, the U.S. should:

- *Lay its cards down on the number of troops it plans to leave in Afghanistan post-2014.* The White House should commit to keeping a fairly robust number of U.S. forces in Afghanistan over the next several years. Former U.S. Central Command chief General James Mattis made clear in recent remarks to Congress that he hoped the U.S. would leave behind around 13,500 troops and that other NATO nations would leave an additional 6,500 troops. This would bring a total of around 20,000 international forces stationed in Afghanistan beyond 2014 to help with training and advising the Afghan forces.

- *Encourage continued strengthening of the democratic process in the country rather than rely on the false hope of political reconciliation with the Taliban.* The Taliban believe they will win the war in Afghanistan without

Hamid Karzai

Hamid Karzai, born 24 December 1957 in Kandahar, Afghanistan, ... was a leader in efforts to reconstitute Afghanistan after the demise of the [radical Islamic government of the] Taliban in 2001. ...

Soon after the 11 September 2001 attacks against the United States, Karzai began to organize a tribal militia to fight the Taliban. ... On 8 October 2001, one day after the United States started bombing the Taliban, he led militia into the Kandahar area. The Taliban almost captured him, but he was rescued by U.S. helicopters. The U.S. government only reluctantly came to see him as a key Pushtun leader. When a body of prominent Afghans assembled in Bonn, Germany, to constitute a new regime, the United States and representatives of the Northern Alliance, now the main political instrument of U.S. policy in Afghanistan, induced the attendees to name him leader of a provisional administration. Installed on 22 December 2001, Karzai's task was to organize a *loya jirga* (national assembly) that would elect a temporary head of state who would form a permanent government. In the summer of 2002 the *loya jirga* elected him president of the Afghan Transitional Authority, commissioning him to draft a new constitution, form a national army, and set up a national election by 2004. As transitional president his main achievement by the summer of 2003 was the securing of commitments from other countries of more than $4 billion for reconstruction. ... There have been several attempts on his life, the most notable on 5 September 2002, when a gunman missed him at point-blank range.

Robert L. Canfield, "Hamid Karzai,"
Encyclopedia of the Modern Middle East,
Global Issues in Context, February 13, 2014.

compromising politically and through violent intimidation of the Afghan population, especially when U.S. and coalition troops are departing. Taliban leaders appear unmotivated to compromise for peace and indeed are stepping up attacks on the Afghan security forces and civilians. The White House should focus on promoting democratic processes and institutions that will directly counter extremist ideologies and practices. Integral to this strategy is supporting a free and fair electoral process next spring both through technical assistance and regular and consistent messaging on the importance of holding the elections on time.

- *Further condition U.S. military aid to Pakistan on its willingness to crack down on Taliban and Haqqani network [an Islamic insurgent group] sanctuaries on its territory.* There continues to be close ties between the Pakistani military and the Taliban leadership and its ally, the Haqqani network, which is responsible for some of the fiercest attacks against coalition and Afghan forces. In early June, the U.S. House of Representatives approved language in the fiscal year 2014 National Defense Authorization Act that conditions reimbursement of Coalition Support Funds (CSF) pending Pakistani actions against the Haqqani network. Hopefully, the language will be retained in the final bill. The U.S. provides CSF funds to reimburse Pakistan for the costs associated with stationing some 100,000 Pakistani troops along the border with Afghanistan. Pakistan has received over $10 billion in CSF funding over the past decade.

Avoid Repeating History

The U.S. should not repeat the same mistake it made 20 years ago by disengaging abruptly from Afghanistan, especially when so much blood and treasure has been expended in the country over the past decade. There is a genuine risk of the Taliban reestablishing its power base and facilitating the revival of [terrorist group] al-Qaeda in the region if the U.S. gives up the mission in Afghanistan.

While frustration with Karzai is high, U.S. officials should not allow a troop drawdown to turn into a rush for the exits that would lead to greater instability in Afghanistan and thus leave the U.S. more vulnerable to the global terrorist threat.

•

"*Iran's interests in Afghanistan coincide with Western objectives.*"

Iran Is Central to Solving the Afghan Conflict

Aaron Ellis

Aaron Ellis is a regular contributor to Egremont, *the official blog of the Tory Reform Group. He also blogs about international relations, with an emphasis on British foreign policy, at* Thinking Strategically. *In the following viewpoint, he argues that Iran has an interest in a stable Afghanistan. However, American animosity toward Iran, based in opposition to Iran's military program, has pushed Iran to support the Taliban and foment conflict in Afghanistan. Ellis argues that Britain should work to repair relations with Iran to help stabilize Afghanistan.*

As you read, consider the following questions:

1. Ellis says that Iranian actions in Afghanistan are not a bid for world mastery. What does he think they are instead?

2. What do Nader and Laha say is the purpose of Iran's asymmetric strategies?

3. What should be Britain's first diplomatic step in regard to Iran, according to Ellis?

One cannot govern well by reacting to events.

Ally with Iran

The British government must share this view, as it is the intention behind the National Security Council [NSC]. It is supposed to put day-to-day crises into a larger context and shape a strategic response to them. Speaking in Washington, DC, several months after the NSC was created, William Hague, the foreign secretary, boasted that it had already made Britain's Afghanistan policy strategically "coherent," among other things.

Yet Britain's handling of Iran suggests that this is not the case. The Iranians ought to be the West's allies in Afghanistan but saber rattling over their nuclear program is forcing them to undermine NATO's [North Atlantic Treaty Organization's] efforts there.

If London really wants to resolve these crises, it needs to adopt a truly strategic approach toward them, not react to them as though they were unrelated events.

It was reported last week [in April 2012] that Iran may have tried to exacerbate anti-American riots in Afghanistan in February, after careless soldiers burned copies of the Quran.

The Tehran regime ordered its agents to "exploit the anticipated public outrage by trying to instigate violent protests in the capital, Kabul, and across the western part of the country, according to American officials," reported the *New York Times*.

The typical reaction to these stories by war hawks is to see Tehran's mischief making as a sinister bid for world mastery, not defensive measures meant to deter Western military action.

When Iranian weapons allegedly destined for the Taliban were seized in Afghanistan last March, then defense secretary Liam Fox said, "This confirms my often repeated view of the dangers that Iran poses not only through its nuclear program but its continuing policy of destabilizing its neighbors."

> Supplying weapons to help the Taliban kill [ISAF (International Security Assistance Force)] soldiers is a clear example of the threat they pose.

In response to a question by Robert Halfon shortly before the Quran riots about Iranian activities in Afghanistan, Hague congratulated the hawkish parliamentarian for assiduously "pointing out the malign influence of Iran on its neighbors in several directions."

The hawk talk about Tehran's mischief making in Afghanistan adds another stroke to the war drums that have been beaten over Iran of late but it actually undermines the government's goals *vis-à-vis* those countries.

It is unlikely that the latter will participate in a regional settlement to end the war if foreign powers persist in viewing them as a malign actor, worsening relations between Tehran and the West and making it harder to negotiate a solution to the nuclear impasse.

Instead of reacting to these crises separately, the British government must adopt a joint approach on them, with sound strategic thinking underpinning it. Such an approach requires a rethink on Iran's role in Afghanistan, recognition that its actions toward one impact the other, and various diplomatic steps to help achieve the goals stated above.

Iran's Interests

Although some of its activities may suggest otherwise, Iran's interests in Afghanistan coincide with Western objectives, which the government must keep in mind. As former diplomat Sherard Cowper-Coles observed correctly in *Cables from*

Kabul: The Inside Story of the West's Afghanistan Campaign, Tehran has "no rational interest in continuing instability in [the country], or in a Taliban victory."

Given this, why do they mischief make? "Iran currently views its interests in Afghanistan through the prism of US-Iranian enmity," write Alireza Nader and Joya Laha in a study for the RAND Corporation.

> Iranian leaders view the US and coalition presence in Afghanistan with great anxiety, especially in light of the US military threats against Iran's nuclear facilities. As it has reportedly been employed in Iraq, Iran's asymmetric strategy would use proxy insurgent forces to tie down and distract the United States from focusing on Iran and its nuclear program, and provides a retaliatory capability in the event of US military action.

Unless Britain rethinks its rhetoric on Iranian interference in Afghanistan—recognizing that it is defensive, not offensive—it will force Tehran to undermine NATO efforts there even further. It can forget a regional settlement underwriting the country's stability after 2014 if it excludes one of the biggest stakeholders.

In addition to a rethink on Iranian behavior, the government needs to take a number of diplomatic steps to restart dialogue between Tehran and London, so that an end to the war in Afghanistan and an end to the nuclear impasse can be negotiated.

First, the United Kingdom should reopen its embassy in Iran. "Without embassies, the basic function of diplomacy—keeping some kind of dialogue going even when views are diametrically opposed—is essentially suspended," the former diplomat and minister Mark Malloch-Brown has written.

This should be followed up by Britain beginning a conversation with Tehran about how it can work with the West in Afghanistan. If it persuades the Iranians to help, not hinder the allies in ending the war, it may be easier to negotiate a solution to their nuclear program, as there will be an element of trust between the parties.

William Hague once said that the National Security Council will not only minimize risks to the United Kingdom but "look for the positive trends in the world, since our security requires seizing opportunity as well as mitigating risk." Yet when it comes to Iran and Afghanistan, the government has emphasized risk over opportunity.

If it wants to achieve its goals for either country, this emphasis needs to change.

"*Both Iran and Saudi Arabia compete to shape Afghan domestic politics and its possible future governance, much of it through attempting to curb the influence of the other.*"

The Saudi-Iranian Rivalry Is Central to the Afghan Conflict

Shahrbanou Tadjbakhsh

Shahrbanou Tadjbakhsh is a research associate with the Peace Research Institute Oslo (PRIO) and the editor of Rethinking the Liberal Peace: External Models and Local Alternatives. *In the following viewpoint, she argues that the rivalry between Saudi Arabia and Iran has strongly affected the conflict in Afghanistan. She says that both countries vie for influence in the region, working to form ties with the Taliban. Saudi Arabia works to advance the interests of Sunni Muslims, while Iran works to advance the interests of Shia Muslims in Afghanistan. She suggests that recognizing the competing efforts of Saudi Arabia and Iran is important to dealing with conflict in Afghanistan.*

As you read, consider the following questions:

1. According to Tadjbakhsh, what government does Saudi Arabia want to see in Afghanistan in the long term?

Shahrbanou Tadjbakhsh, "The Persian Gulf and Afghanistan: Iran and Saudi Arabia's Rivalry Projected," Peace Research Institute Oslo, March 2013. Copyright © 2013 by Shahrbanou Tadjbakhsh. Reproduced by permission.

2. What does Tadjbakhsh say is Iran's main concern in terms of the political process in Afghanistan?

3. What geographic factors give Iran leverage over Afghanistan, and which give Afghanistan leverage over Iran, according to Tadjbakhsh?

While Iran shares closer cultural, historical and geographic affinities with Afghanistan, Saudi Arabia has not stood idle. Both Iran and Saudi Arabia compete to shape Afghan domestic politics and its possible future governance, much of it through attempting to curb the influence of the other. They do so by using their connections with various ethnic and religious groups, propagating their distinct religious doctrines, increasing economic ties and attempting to influence insurgent groups. At the same time, they seek legitimacy and relevance by manoeuvring to become part of the solution to the Afghan security problem: Saudi Arabia tries to increase its bargaining power through careful funding for the Taliban [Islamic militant group] and influencing the insurgency through Pakistan. Iran openly stands against the presence of foreign troops in Afghanistan, while billing itself as a neighbour with natural, long-standing ties without which a solution for Afghanistan cannot be found. By doing so, it proactively tries to reverse its isolation from where it has been forcibly and symbolically located, a decade ago, on 'the axis of evil' [referring to Iran, Iraq, and North Korea].

Effects of a Rivalry

Saudi Arabia is strategically interested in preventing Iran's influence in Afghanistan while keeping itself relevant as an ally to the main actor in the Afghan terrain, the United States. In the long term, it wants to see an Islamic Sunni government in Afghanistan. However, neither does Saudi Arabia today appear to have significant influence over the Taliban's [leadership, the] Quetta Shura, nor does the kingdom have a coordinated foreign and aid policy towards Afghanistan. It is in the Afghan terrain that Iran can gain recognition as a key regional actor with its economic and cultural leadership and where it could, given its common interest with the USA, see potential for constructive dialogue. Furthermore, Iran would like to prevent Afghanistan, with its long and lawless border, from becoming a source of intensified narcotics or gun trafficking. In the final analysis, Iran is concerned that Afghan soil will be used as a platform from which its territory is attacked by NATO or US forces. Iran also hopes that an eventual Pashtun-led government would include a fair representation by non-Pashtun ethnic minorities. As a result, even though Iran is against the US presence in the region, it does not want to completely jeopardize the coalition's stabilization efforts given that a total collapse of the [Afghan president Hamid] Karzai government would not be in its interest. Instead, it sends signals of its relevance to the USA and its allies: It can provide extensive experience and cooperation on curbing the production and trafficking of narcotics and provide access to NATO supply routes through its port at Chabahar. Yet, it could also play the role of spoiler by potentially using its extensive influence over different groups if its interests are not taken into account.

Aid and Influence

How has the Saudi-Iranian rivalry impacted concretely on the involvement of these two countries in Afghanistan? . . .

1) *The politics and practice of aid.* Both countries have been generous donors. The impact of Saudi funding in Afghanistan is difficult to extrapolate as money flows from numerous sources in Saudi Arabia to various destinations in Afghanistan. Iran, despite its economic difficulties, has proven a more consistent and efficient donor. However, most of Iranian investment has gone into the Western province of Herat. Under heavy sanctions, Iran seeks to develop alternative routes for trade and investment. If stability ensues in Afghanistan,

Iran could carve out a role for itself in reconstruction by providing linkages to central Asia and Pakistan. In case the situation worsens, it would at least have created an autonomous buffer zone to protect its investments in the western part of Afghanistan.

2) *Influence on the political process and negotiations with the Taliban.* Past relations have made Saudi Arabia a prime candidate for facilitating negotiations between the Taliban and the Karzai government. Since the first public attempt to bring them together in 2008 and periodic pleas by President Karzai for Saudi mediation notwithstanding, efforts have not led to any breakthrough. This could be because of the waning influence of the kingdom on the Quetta Shura, or the mistrust of the western coalition about Saudi motivations and designs in the future of Afghanistan (not least given its rivalry with Iran). Iran by contrast was predisposed to disfavour any openings with the Sunni extremist group that had been particularly hostile during its reign. Yet, while Iran has repeatedly objected to the 'Talibanization' of Afghanistan, its main concern is the permanent presence of foreign troops in the neighbouring country, and the potential use of Afghan soil by US forces to conduct attacks on its territory. This concern, together with a pragmatic approach that dictates a new view of the Taliban as potential players in the future of Afghanistan, has meant that Iran has gradually developed contacts with them. Unlike Saudi Arabia, which has not made attempts to go beyond its traditional allies, Iran's strategy has been to develop a multi-player policy in Afghanistan in order to exploit all available options.

Ethnicity and Religion

3) *Support for ethnic groups*, with a sub-text of a Sunni/Shia rift, is a third area where the rivalry between the two gets projected onto Afghanistan. Saudi Arabia's actions are informed by its Wahhabi (Salafist) Sunni ideology, making it weary of the threat of sectarianism and of Shia domination. In Af-

ghanistan, this translates into support to those that would ensure the enforcement of an Islamic morale of governance and
the establishment of the Sharia [Islamic law] as the basis of
legislation in the country. In the current political scene, such
an ideology is mainly pursued by the Taliban or the Hezbi-
Islami, both of whom find their main support base among the
Pashtuns. By extension, Saudi Arabia has cultivated very little
contacts with other ethnic minority groups, even Sunni Tajiks,
for their perceived closeness with Iran given their common
language. Iranian support for ethnic groups in Afghanistan
stems from three ambitions: First, to exploit cultural and lin-
guistic affinity for increased influence; second, to ensure that
Shia minorities are treated adequately, as Iran has historically
considered itself as the guardian of Shiism worldwide; and
third, to strengthen and unite the Shia Hazaras and the Tajik
Persian speakers, which combined could comprise some 45%
of the population, as a counterweight to anti-Iranian, pro-
Saudi, pro-Pakistani elements among Afghan Pashtuns. While
Iran supports the establishment of a multi-ethnic government
with an independent foreign policy, friendly towards Iran, it
realizes that Afghanistan will most likely remain under
Pashtun-led government. Hence, it advocates for national reconciliation and ensuring of power sharing among ethnic minorities through a secular system.

4) *The religious competition* has been symbolized by the
construction of the two large mosques in Kabul, one supported in 2006 partly by Iran, the other expected to start in
2013 with Saudi funding. Saudi Arabia seeks a government in
Afghanistan that would enforce a strict Islamic moral. Iranians, by contrast, advocate for a secular government that protects the rights of minorities. This has to do with the fact that
multiculturalism and multiethnicity are reality in Iran more
than they are in Saudi Arabia. Yet, although Iran has pursued
a strategy of supporting minorities, both Shia and Sunni, this
is not to say that it has not lent particular attention to its co-
religious 'brothers'.

5) *Geographic contiguity*: Geography, and by extension the potential spillover of threats across borders, is an added element which explains Iran's extensive interest in Afghanistan beyond mere rivalry with Saudi Arabia. Common borders raise issues such as trafficking of illicit drugs, sharing of water resources, as well as migration of refugees and workers. As Iran has been directly affected by the sharp increase in drug consumption among its youth and because its territory provides the main route for exporting Afghan narcotics to the West, it is sharply critical of the coalition's failure to curb production. It is also concerned with the uncontrolled connection between drug smuggling and terrorism in the border area where Iran, Afghanistan and Pakistan meet. Furthermore, the potentially serious problem of water sharing of the Helmand River gives Kabul leverage over Iran, making the latter vulnerable and dependent on decisions made in Afghanistan. The refugee issue, by contrast, gives leverage to Iran: Although the large number of Afghan refugees and migrant workers pose a challenge for integration and employment in Iran, they are used by Iran to influence decision making in Kabul and as a tool to further the country's quest for recognition.

Periodical and Internet Sources Bibliography

The following articles have been selected to supplement the diverse views presented in this chapter.

Hashmat Baktash and Shashank Bengali	"Taliban Threatens to Attack Presidential Election in Afghanistan," *Los Angeles Times*, March 10, 2014.
David S. Cloud	"Afghanistan Security at Risk in U.S. Pullout, Official Says," *Los Angeles Times*, February 27, 2014.
John-Thor Dahlburg	"NATO: No Afghan Deal, No Troops Past 2014," *Huffington Post*, February 26, 2014.
Karen DeYoung	"U.S. Examines Afghanistan Option That Would Leave Behind 3,000 Troops," *Washington Post*, February 23, 2014.
Kathy Gannon and Rahim Faiez	"Karzai Says Afghanistan Doesn't Need U.S. Troops to Stay Past End of Year," *Washington Post*, March 15, 2014.
Emma Graham-Harrison	"One in Four Afghans Has Lost Someone to Violence in Past Year, Says Charity," *Guardian*, February 25, 2014.
Rod Nordland	"Attacks on Aid Workers Rise in Afghanistan, U.N. Says," *New York Times*, December 2, 2013.
Kevin Sieff	"In Model Afghan City, Kidnappings Surge," *Washington Post*, April 24, 2013.
Dylan Welch	"Afghanistan Mass Kidnapping: Gunmen Abduct Dozens of Workers Clearing Landmines in Herat Province," *Huffington Post*, January 21, 2014.

OPPOSING
VIEWPOINTS®
SERIES

CHAPTER 2

What Issues Confront Afghan Democracy?

Chapter Preface

Dr. Abdullah Abdullah is one of the most important political figures in Afghanistan. He was part of the Afghanistan resistance to the Taliban in the 1990s and served in the Afghan government in exile when the Taliban took control of the country. After the American invasion, he served as Afghan foreign minister from 2002 to 2006, according to his biography at TasvirAfghanistan.com.

Abdullah ran as a candidate for Afghanistan's 2009 presidential election against incumbent Hamid Karzai. The vote count for the election put Abdullah in second place next to Karzai. Massive vote fraud led to the discarding of many votes, especially for Karzai, with the result that neither candidate achieved more than 50 percent of the vote. Karzai only received 48.2 percent, though many suspected that even that total was inflated by fraud and corruption. According to the Afghan Constitution, if no candidate received more than half of the vote, a second round of voting was required between the two lead candidates, in this case Karzai and Abdullah.

A second election, however, would be expensive, and the problems with fraud in the first round made many feel the results of the second election could not be legitimate. According to Jon Boone in a November 1, 2009, article in the *Guardian*, Abdullah hoped to negotiate a power-sharing deal with Karzai. Boone quotes an official as saying, "Abdullah's demands were low—he would have taken a job as head of the constitutional reform committee in order to meet his campaign pledges. But Karzai wasn't interested." Convinced a second election would be neither free nor fair, Abdullah decided not to contest the second round. Karzai won the election by default, though his legitimacy remained in question for many.

Abdullah again ran for the presidency in April 2014. Hamid Karzai was term limited and could not run, leaving a field of eleven other candidates. Polling is difficult in Afghanistan, and in a February 2, 2014, article at NPR, Sean Carberry discusses experts' predictions that Abdullah would be one of the top two candidates, that no one candidate would win 50 percent of the vote, and that Abdullah would therefore compete in a runoff election.

These predictions proved correct. After the April 2014 election, the two frontrunners, Abdullah and Ashraf Ghani, a former finance minister, prepared for a runoff election in June 2014. Karzai, though not running, still has much influence in Afghanistan, including possibly the ability to affect the polls through fraud, as he seems to have done in the past. He opposes Abdullah and prefers Ghani. As of early September 2014, results of the runoff election were unknown.

The remainder of this chapter examines other issues affecting Afghan democracy, including corruption and whether Afghanistan is culturally able to support democratic institutions.

> *"The new constitution gave Afghanistan its first-ever highly centralised government. Given the country's ethnic and regional divides, that was a recipe for instability."*

Banyan: Not a Pleasant Prospect

The Economist

The Economist *is a British weekly newsmagazine focusing on business and politics. The following viewpoint argues that the democratic process in Afghanistan is weak and that the 2014 elections are unlikely to be fair. The elections also include many candidates with murky pasts and links to war crimes. The* Economist *says that the democratic problems are largely caused by the way the government was set up by Western governments following the overthrow of the Taliban in 2001. Among the mistakes were the exclusion of all Taliban factions and the inclusion of anti-Taliban warlords with a history of abuses.*

As you read, consider the following questions:

1. According to the *Economist*, what did Hamid Karzai say that showed a lack of gratitude to NATO?

2. Who is Abdul Rasul Sayyaf?

3. Why is Hamid Karzai unlikely to endorse a candidate, according to the *Economist?*

Leaders of the NATO-led alliance known as ISAF that is fighting in Afghanistan might be expected to be glad to see the back of President Hamid Karzai. The man whose government they have supported since 2001 is ineligible to stand in the election next April. Fickle and moody, Mr Karzai this week showed again just how ungrateful he can be. "The entire NATO exercise", he told the BBC, "was one that caused Afghanistan a lot of suffering, a lot of loss of life, and no gains because the country is not secure." Nearly 3,400 ISAF soldiers have been killed defending Mr Karzai's government from its enemies. Western commanders were understandably indignant.

Two factors, however, tempered their outrage. First, they know that when the West installed Mr Karzai, it saddled him with all the forms of democracy. Their man has therefore had to show that he is serving Afghans, not foreign generals. Second, after a frantic scramble for presidential candidates to register by October 6th, they know that in a year's time they may be looking wistfully back on the Karzai era. Whoever succeeds him may be even harder to deal with, have a more dubious background and have achieved power by even murkier means than those that saw Mr Karzai "re-elected" in 2009.

Mr Karzai will stand down in the year when ISAF is to withdraw its combat troops, leaving the Afghan army to carry on the fight against Taliban insurgents. The West is naturally anxious to leave behind a government that is capable of surviving and that has a semblance of democratic legitimacy. A president respected at home and abroad would certainly help.

Some 27 candidates have registered, each with two vice-presidential running mates in tow. Not all these men are warlords, and many will drop out. But enough are tribal strongmen with tainted records to cast a dark shadow over the entire field. Tickets often bridge ethnic divides, with at least one member of the largest group, the Pushtuns. One prominent candidate, Abdul Rasul Sayyaf, is credited with having invited al-Qaeda's leadership to set up shop in Afghanistan. Another, Gul Agha Sherzai, is a warlord from Kandahar, once the stronghold of the (largely Pushtun) Taliban. He is nicknamed the "Bulldozer"—a tribute to his personal style as much as to his track record in seeing projects completed as governor of the province of Nangarhar.

One vice-presidential candidate, Abdul Rashid Dostum, is a leader of the Uzbek minority and hence an important vote winner, a role he performed for Mr Karzai in 2009. He was a military commander in the days of the Soviet-backed government that fell to the Taliban in 1994 and a warlord with a fearsome reputation. He is said by Western diplomats who have spent time with him recently to have mellowed. This is just as well, since he is on the ticket of one of the more cerebral candidates, Ashraf Ghani, who once called him a "known killer". Mr Ghani is a former finance minister and World Bank official, and co-author of books, appropriately enough, on "fixing failed states" and "strategies for state-building".

Another of the more cosmopolitan candidates, Abdullah Abdullah, has similarly teamed up with two rougher diamonds. [Jan] Mohammad Khan is a leader of the Hezb-i-Islami party, whose military wing is part of the insurgency fighting the government. Mohammad Mohaqiq, from the Hazara minority, has survived four recent attempts on his life. Like Mr Dostum, he was accused in a report last year by a human-rights watchdog of war crimes before 2001.

Dr Abdullah, an ethnic Tajik (though with Pushtun blood), was foreign minister for the Northern Alliance, which, with American air and special-forces support, toppled the Taliban in 2001. He then emerged as an opposition leader and was runner-up in the fraudulent election in 2009.

Afghanistan's 2010 Elections

The September 2010 elections [in Afghanistan] were marked by decreased popular participation and profound irregularities, including far more electoral cards than the number of registered voters, intimidation and ballot stuffing, and fraud in vote counts, leading the IEC [Independent Election Committee of Afghanistan] to reject some 25 percent of the voting cards. The combination of insecurity in many Pashtun provinces and the clever manipulation of the SNTV [single non-transferable vote] system by well-organized minorities led to the Pashtun losing some 20 seats in the lower house of parliament, further decreasing the president's hold on parliament and leading him to encourage the Supreme Court to set up a special tribunal to adjudicate election complaints, despite its broadly acknowledged lack of jurisdiction in this area. While parliament was eventually convened on 25 January 2011 with its membership intact, the Special Tribunal remains in place as a kind of Damocles' sword over the lower house, presumably to encourage its members to be more accommodating towards the president's wishes. What is clear is that the 2010 parliamentary elections have brought the three main organs of the state into even greater disrepute, bringing their legitimacy into question. . . .

Francesc Vendrell,
"Elections and the Future of Afghanistan,"
in Elections in Dangerous Places:
Democracy and the Paradoxes of Peacebuilding.
Ed. David Gillies. Quebec, Canada:
McGill-Queen's University Press, 2011, pp. 30–31.

This election is unlikely to be much fairer. An article by Martine van Bijlert of the Afghan Analysts Network, a respected research group, lists the problems: a defective voter registry; millions of available voter cards not linked to voters; widespread insecurity; and "the collusion of electoral and security staff, whether prompted by loyalty, money or pressure, at all levels".

The sense that the state has the power to sway the election result gives great weight to any endorsement Mr Karzai might make. Yet he is likely to keep his promise not to offer one—at least openly—even though the field includes his older brother and a former foreign minister believed to be a favourite. Endorsement would taint the victory of "his" candidate; or, should the candidate lose, cause grave embarrassment to Mr Karzai. But he is not going away. A grand residence is under construction next to the presidential palace in Kabul. Mr Karzai says he wants to stay in the country and enjoy his "legacy". Yet his presence may prove unhelpful, and his relations with his successor fraught.

Design Flaws

Looking at the mess the election is likely to be, outsiders may be inclined to conclude that Afghans are not ready for democracy. Yet their political system was subverted from the outset by dubious choices made in 2001. For one, Mr Karzai himself has proved both weak and high-handed, and has tolerated scandalous corruption while always blaming foreigners.

The new constitution gave Afghanistan its first-ever highly centralised government. Given the country's ethnic and regional divides, that was a recipe for instability. In retrospect it was also a mistake to let into government warlords who had fought the Taliban but who were notorious for past abuses. And leaving even moderate elements of the Taliban outside the political process altogether led them to regroup as an insurgency. The steady escalation of the war might have happened anyway. But the exclusion of the Taliban made it inevitable. So the political structure agreed in 2001 never really gave peace, or democracy, a chance.

"This election will not make the winner legitimate in the eyes of the Afghan people because democratic elections aren't a source of legitimacy in Afghanistan and Afghan politics."

Afghanistan's Culture Does Not Support Democracy

Thomas H. Johnson as told to Greg Bruno

Thomas H. Johnson is the director of culture and conflict studies at the Naval Postgraduate School. Greg Bruno is a staff writer for the Council on Foreign Relations. In the following viewpoint, Johnson argues that Afghanistan does not have a tradition of representative democracy and that national elections cannot produce a legitimate ruler. He says that America's efforts to create American-style democratic institutions quickly are doomed to fail and are a sign of American arrogance.

As you read, consider the following questions:

1. What does Johnson say is the "big quote" that is applicable to democracy in Afghanistan?

2. What does Johnson think should have been done instead of a runoff election?

3. What do you need to have for a successful counterinsurgency strategy, according to Johnson?

After weeks of high-level diplomacy between Washington and Kabul, Afghan president Hamid Karzai agreed to a November 7 [2009] runoff election with his main challenger, Abdullah Abdullah. World leaders, from U.S. president Barack Obama to UN [United Nations] secretary-general Ban Ki-moon, praised the decision. But Afghanistan expert Thomas H. Johnson of the Naval Postgraduate School says the runoff election—agreed to after intense lobbying from U.S. officials—will not produce a legitimate leader in the eyes of Afghan voters. Instead, Johnson says, the runoff could further destabilize the country, especially if Abdullah wins. "There's almost an American arrogance here thinking that we could come in and install Jeffersonian representative democracy on this country," Johnson says. He says the Obama administration should seek to rely more on Afghan systems of governance which, while unrecognizable to Western institutions, have been "able to resolve disputes such as this through consensus" for centuries.

Painting Democracy on Afghanistan

Greg Bruno: Before President Karzai's decision to stand for a runoff on November 7, there had been much discussion as to whether the Obama administration needed to wait to move on its strategy until the election results were official. Is a credible Afghan government a prerequisite for Washington to move forward?

Thomas Johnson: The big quote is "democracies make elections, elections don't make democracies." This is especially the case in Afghanistan, which we've tried to paint democracy on over the last eight years since the Bonn Agreement [which created the country's post-Taliban government in 2001]. In many respects, talking about the strategy and reevaluating the strategy before we have final election results is missing the larger point. This election will not make the winner legitimate in the eyes of the Afghan people because democratic elections aren't a source of legitimacy in Afghanistan and Afghan politics. The current debate is primarily a reflection of U.S. cultural and political mirror imaging on Afghanistan. [In pushing for a runoff, the Obama administration] may have opened up a can of worms. I was in Afghanistan and saw the fraud three or four months ago. I knew this was going to be a fraudulent election. If by chance Abdullah Abdullah won a runoff, that's the makings of a civil war in the country. I'm not sure that all of these variables have come into place in the decision calculation in Washington right now. There's no question that Karzai had a fraudulent election, but one, either way these results will not make a legitimate ruler and two, the possibilities of an overturn of the Karzai regime has implications that are very problematic. I do not think this election is going to result in a legitimate leader one way or the other.

American Arrogance

Afghanistan has long relied on other forms of decision making, like jirgas and councils. It sounds like you're suggesting the Western definition of democracy does not translate to Afghanistan.

[The Obama administration is] grasping at straws to try to find legitimate political players in Afghanistan that they can work with on the political side as well as the military side.

Anybody that knows the history of Afghanistan will recognize the fact that they've practiced pure Greek democracy at the village level for two millennia. There's almost an American arrogance here thinking that we could come in and install Jeffersonian representative democracy on this country. It's also extremely important to recognize that the entire election fiasco of August has [set] any type of movement toward democracy back in Afghanistan. What do you think the Afghans are thinking about who went to the polls, in some cases risking their well-being and the well-being of their family? Now they're waiting to hear what's going to happen two months later. My final point is that if we're going to have a special election for city council in Boise, Idaho, you couldn't pull it off in two weeks. What makes America and Washington think that they could have a credible rerun of this election process in a two-week period?

Many analysts thought Karzai would refuse calls for a runoff. Any idea why he changed his mind?

I said publicly on numerous occasions that there'd be no way there could be a runoff election and that Karzai would claim sovereignty and wouldn't allow the UN election commission to play such a role. Of course, his independent election commission was completely handpicked. I was surprised [at his decision to agree to a runoff]. I can't speak with authority, but I would imagine that there was some pretty big arm-twisting going on behind the scenes by the United States, ISAF [International Security Assistance Force], and NATO [North Atlantic Treaty Organization]. This is all being done under the assumption that this is going to create some type of legitimacy for the winner of this runoff election. That's where I have basic problems.

What was the better approach here?

In the ideal world, I would have liked to see more of an emergency loya jirga [a temporary council traditionally made up of representatives from Afghan tribes and opposing factions used to decide matters of national significance]. I would have liked to see an emergency loya jirga with 1,500 to 2,000 delegates representing all of the major players and parts of the countries to have them resolve this the way they traditionally resolve these types of problems in the past. When push comes to shove, we should have relied on the historical processes that Afghans relied on in the past.

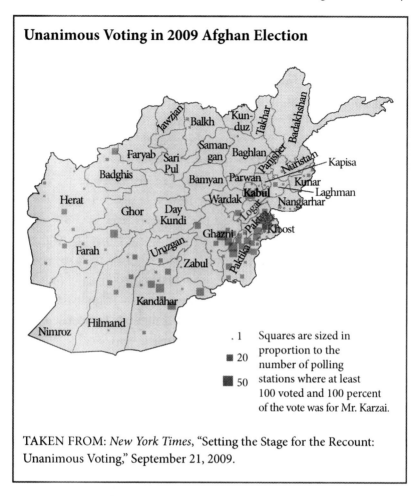

Unanimous Voting in 2009 Afghan Election

.1

■ 20

■ 50

Squares are sized in proportion to the number of polling stations where at least 100 voted and 100 percent of the vote was for Mr. Karzai.

TAKEN FROM: *New York Times*, "Setting the Stage for the Recount: Unanimous Voting," September 21, 2009.

No Legitimacy

How does this play in the Afghan street? It's been portrayed by Obama and Secretary of State [Hillary] Clinton as a victory for democracy.

The average Afghan in the hinterland regions—remember that this is a country that's primarily 75 to 80 percent rural—really doesn't have a real clear idea of what's going on. We continue to mirror image our solutions onto Afghanistan; because they've asked for a runoff election this is a great victory for democracy? I don't buy that at all. And if it was a great victory for democracy, why don't we try to have the election more systematically done rather than say, arbitrarily, that it's going to be within two weeks. I recognize that there are winners coming out and other dynamics, but if we were really serious about this why would it matter if we waited two or three months? The response for that is this is all outside the Afghan constitution. There's no procedure in the constitution for a lag structure like this before the next election and who's going to be running the show. But I'm really concerned that we think we can just pull off a new election in two weeks. Let's not forget that just a couple of years ago in 2005 when they had the Wolesi Jirga, the legislative elections in Afghanistan, the United Nations publicly stated that they were the most complicated elections in the history of man. Now this isn't as complicated as legislative elections in Afghanistan, but it's still a fairly complicated process. I'm very concerned that we say we can turn around and do this in two weeks.

This [runoff] election will not make the winner legitimate in the eyes of the Afghan people because democratic elections aren't a source of legitimacy in Afghanistan and Afghan politics.

Among the pieces of evidence cited as fraud after the August 20 vote are claims that entire precincts or districts voted for one candidate, in many cases Karzai. Couldn't that simply have been the will of the tribal structure in that region, and not fraud?

Probably most of that was fraudulent. One of the real problems with this election was that hundreds of polling places sent in ballots that were never opened to the public. But you're absolutely correct. I detailed the analysis of the presidential election of 2004 and found a high propensity of Afghans to vote along ethno-linguistic affinities: The Pashtun were voting for Karzai last time, the Tajiks were for [Yunus] Qanuni, the Hazaras were voting for [Mohammad] Mohaqiq, and the Uzbeks were voting for [Abdul Rashid] Dostum. I found very clear and convincing statistical evidence of that. I obviously haven't done that type of analysis on this past election, but for the ballots that weren't fraudulent I wouldn't be surprised if you see those similar types of dynamics.

Looking for a US Strategy

I recently spoke with an election expert who monitored the first round of voting, and plans to return to monitor the November 7 runoff. His assessment was that it's all about security this time. What's more important in your mind, access to polling sites or producing a legitimate winner?

It's not possible to talk about legitimacy. I'm very dubious at this stage of Afghan history and "democratic" development that an election makes a legitimate leader. In many respects, that's not at all the case. We're just kidding ourselves to think that this next election is going to result in some type of legitimate Afghan leader. Max Weber, the famous sociologist, talked about three forms of regime legitimacy: traditional (which was often patriarchal or dynastic), religious, and Western/rational. For two millennia, Afghanistan or the area where Afghanistan now occupies, has determined legitimacy by the first two sources of legitimacy. That the United States, UN, and NATO think they can change this in a short period of time borders on delusional thinking. Let's not forget that it took 150 years if not longer for the United States to have universal women's suffrage. But for some reason we think we can have these types of institutions take hold overnight in a country that has never had a history of anything resembling Jeffersonian representative democracy.

So perhaps the runoff plan was simply a way to sell it to the U.S. public, to maintain support for the war?

That's part of it, but there's inertia going on here. We've developed so much of our strategy and certain policies based on historical assumptions. Some of these carry through with this administration. Of course, the second inaugural speech by George W. Bush talked about his legacy of developing democratic regimes worldwide. There's also inertia taking place here, and we haven't really sat back and reevaluated what some of our assumptions are concerning legitimacy and rule in Afghanistan.

But isn't that what the Obama administration is doing, reevaluating its strategy?

Obama gave his strategy in his speech in March, although some statements coming out of the administration seem a little different right now. To ultimately be successful in COIN [counterinsurgency], you've got to have a regime that's viewed as legitimate by 80 percent to 85 percent of the people. I didn't say popular. It doesn't have to be popular, but it does have to be legitimate for COIN to succeed. That's the real dilemma that the Obama administration is facing. They're grasping at straws to try to find legitimate political players in Afghanistan that they can work with on the political side as well as the military side. That's been very difficult.

| *"Societal transformation here is a direct result of the free media."*

The Growth of Media Shows Progress in Afghan Democracy

Associated Press

The Associated Press is a news service. The following viewpoint reports on the growth of Afghanistan's free press, which is covering the 2014 election and broadcasting television debates. Afghan television also broadcasts sporting events and includes female announcers, in contravention of religious conservative dogma. It is uncertain whether the new free media will survive after the United States and coalition forces leave the country, but some are optimistic that the tradition of media freedom established will persist and help Afghanistan build a democracy.

As you read, consider the following questions:

1. According to the viewpoint, how many media outlets are there in Afghanistan?

2. What percentage of Afghans listen to radio and television, according to the viewpoint?

3. What financial challenges do the media outlets in Afghanistan face after the coalition forces leave?

"It's just technical difficulties," explains Mujahid Kakar, the Tolo anchor and moderator of the upcoming debate among six of the main contenders vying to succeed President Hamid Karzai in the April 5 [2014] election.

The moment is a reminder of the difficulties of reporting in an impoverished country torn by war. Yet, in many ways, Afghan media coverage of the crucial campaign that kicked off this week resembles what you'd see in any other modern democracy, with newspaper candidate profiles and political talk shows on numerous TV and radio stations.

A Televised Debate

And this week, for the first time, major contenders for the presidency will introduce themselves to the nation in a televised debate.

The proliferation of Afghan media in the past 12 years is one of the most visible bright spots of the fraught project to foster a stable democracy, even as the NATO [North Atlantic Treaty Organization] military mission in Afghanistan nears its end with the country still riven by war with Taliban insurgents and mired in corruption and poverty.

Given that the [militant Islamic] Taliban [who controlled Afghanistan until 2001] banned television as sinful and allowed only one religious radio station before they were driven from power in 2001, the sheer number of media outlets— dozens of TV channels, more than 100 radio stations and hundreds of newspapers—is stunning. That they are mostly free to set their own agenda is even more so.

"It goes against some of that common wisdom that it's all doomed," says [Ahmad] Nader Nadery, chairman of the Free and Fair Election Foundation, an Afghan pro-democracy group.

Where the Taliban banned sports, Afghans can now watch soccer matches on television. Where music aside from religious hymns was forbidden, there are *American Idol*–style singing competitions. Women were once erased from public life; now some host television shows.

What's less clear is what the future holds for all these media outlets after this year, when most foreign troops will go home and much of the billions in aid dollars is expected to be reduced.

For now, though, Afghan news outlets are enjoying a moment in the sun. Newspapers in Dari and Pashto, the country's main languages, are full of campaign coverage. Radio and TV stations from all over the spectrum—private for-profit ventures, aid-supported democracy boosters and stations supported by political parties or religious groups—compete to offer their views of the race.

Tolo TV

Tolo TV, Afghanistan's most popular channel, is touting the debate as the first in the country to pit all the major presidential candidates against one another. State television hosted a debate between Karzai and two challengers during the last election, in 2009, but it excluded Karzai's main challenger Abdullah Abdullah, who is running again this year. Tolo TV held its own debate in 2009, but Karzai declined to attend.

"It's a historic debate for the country and for the people," says Kakar, 42, a former refugee who studied journalism in Pakistan and returned home after the U.S.-led military intervention. "This is a process of democracy. We prove to the people that these candidates, they have the responsibility toward the people."

It may be a first but probably won't be the last. With Karzai ineligible to serve another term and a wide field of candidates looking to distinguish themselves, debates are expected to be a fixture of the two-month campaign period.

US-Supported Media in Afghanistan

The US embassy in Kabul is demonstrating some smart media initiative by supporting the creation of new TV programs with the right messages. For instance, *Eagle Four*, about a fictional police unit, reports the *Wall Street Journal*, is "the first of several television shows funded by the US government as part of a strategy to galvanize Afghans behind their security forces. The show's first episodes debuted on Tolo TV, one of Afghanistan's largest stations. Tolo will follow up with *Birth of an Army*, a reality show that follows recruits from their first training missions to their battles with insurgents." To illustrate what can be accomplished, Pakistan has already begun to air a similar TV action series dramatizing the role of the Pakistani armed forces in fighting the Taliban called *Beyond the Call of Duty*. It has proven to be very popular, especially with the rural population. As one viewer said, "Most people, including me, initially thought Pakistan was fighting a US war. But when I watched the drama, I came to the conclusion that those guys [i.e., the terrorists] are a cancer for the whole country and should be cut out."

"The US-backed shows are part of a broad allied effort to counter a Taliban propaganda offensive against coalition and Afghan forces, a push that runs parallel to the surge of forces on the ground. TV is seen as an effective way for the United States to spread its message to Afghanistan's largely young and illiterate population. A cop show appeals to the core demographic: impressionable young men."

Robert Reilly, "Shaping Strategic Communications,"
Afghan Endgames: Strategy and Policy Choices for
America's Longest War. *Eds. Hy Rothstein and John Arquilla.*
Washington DC: Georgetown University Press, 2012, p. 183.

With Afghanistan's low literacy levels, radio and television dominate the media landscape, with 63 percent of all Afghans listening to radio regularly and 48 percent watching television, according to research conducted in 2010 for the U.S. Agency for International Development.

Tolo TV—which is part of the privately held Moby Group founded by Afghan-Australian brothers in part with U.S. aid money and is now earning revenue of some $20 million—is by far the most popular channel, with an estimated 10 million viewers tuning in to its mixture of news, sports and light entertainment.

Other television outlets included Ariana and YakTV, which air a mixture of cooking shows, games and Afghan cultural fare. The government is still a major player, with a state television station and more than 30 government-linked radio stations. There are also numerous private stations funded by politicians and religious leaders.

Will a Free Press Last?

While most of Afghanistan's television fare is tame by Western standards—female reporters wear head scarves, and imported Turkish soap operas are pixelated to mask any show of skin by women—the flourishing entertainment and news have drawn the ire of many religious conservatives.

Sadaf Amiri, 23, anchor of a political talk show on Tolo, knows that firsthand from the threats and the cold shoulders from some of the more conservative politicians she has interviewed.

"For a woman, working in the media is a threat in itself, whether someone threatens us personally or not," Amiri says. "But I have been threatened."

Whether the relatively free press will remain in Afghanistan is not certain. Even if the election goes smoothly, Afghanistan's religious conservatives still wield tremendous power, and there is no guarantee that future governments will be able to resist pressure to curtail the press.

A greater threat might be financial. Many of the newly minted stations and newspapers are dependent on foreign funding, and the few profitable private outlets, like Tolo, get much of their advertising revenue from businesses that rely on the coalition.

Still, Nadery argues that this year's unprecedented level of campaign coverage illustrates that Afghanistan has changed in fundamental ways in the past 12 years. Taking a more optimistic view than many, he says Afghans have become accustomed to the new, relatively freewheeling media and won't give it up easily. The same may also go for elections.

"Societal transformation here is a direct result of the free media," Nadery says. "The media also changed the way politics have been done in this country."

"It is time we stop focusing on Afghans and start looking in the mirror."

US Policy Is Responsible for High Levels of Corruption in Afghanistan

Anthony H. Cordesman

Anthony H. Cordesman holds the Arleigh A. Burke Chair in Strategy at the Center for Strategic and International Studies (CSIS) and is a national security analyst on a number of global conflicts. In the following viewpoint, he argues that negligent US policy is responsible for massive corruption in Afghanistan. He says that defense contractors and aid agencies have failed to properly account for funds. In addition, such policies, as failing to fund Afghan police forces, led police to take advantage of opportunities for illegal income. He concludes that US failures have had a devastating effect on the people of Afghanistan.

As you read, consider the following questions:

1. According to Cordesman, where does the bulk of money in Afghanistan go?

Anthony H. Cordesman, "How America Corrupted Afghanistan: Time to Look in the Mirror," CSIS, September 8, 2010. http://csis.org/publication/how-america-corrupted -afghanistan-time-look-mirror. Copyright © 2010 by Center for Strategic and International Studies. All rights reserved. Reproduced by permission.

2. In Cordesman's view, how does the US-supported Afghan Constitution enable corruption?

3. Why did corruption become "existential necessity" in Afghanistan, according to Cordesman?

There is a massive difference between the kind of relatively low-cost corruption, fees, and charges that Afghans have paid in the past and the level of corruption in today's Afghanistan. Afghanistan has always had a large black economy, and Afghan officials, the military, and police have long taken bribes or charged illegal fees. Like at least two-thirds of the countries in the world, this has long been the way the Afghan government and economy operate.

What is different from the past is the sheer scale of today's corruption. Virtually all Afghans believe it cripples the government, creates a small group of ultra-rich power brokers and officials at the expense of the people, and empowers a far less corrupt Taliban by default.

Floods of Uncontrolled Contractor Money

It is time we stop focusing on Afghans and start looking in the mirror. A tiny elite of Afghan officials, senior officers, and power brokers have become vastly wealthy through corruption largely thanks to outside military and aid efforts led by the United States. At the same time, virtually all Afghans in public life—and particularly in government and the police—have become more corrupt for the same reasons.

As SIGAR [Special Inspector General for Afghanistan Reconstruction] and the [Government] Accountability Office (GAO) have made painfully clear, the U.S., other countries, the UN [United Nations], and NGOs [nongovernmental organizations] have poured money into Afghanistan with miserable fiscal controls, little real effort to validate whether such spending levels are necessary, an almost total lack of meaningful transparency, and no meaningful measures of their effectiveness or the level of corruption and waste in such spending.

There is no way to quantify just how much of this money has been wasted, stolen, or diverted. The bulk of the money has gone to military operations, not aid, and there is no meaningful accounting of how the money actually spent affects Afghans or of the nature of the fiscal and accounting practices used by the U.S. or allied forces. It is clear that much of this money goes to U.S. contractors who fail to control their own costs and pass money on to foreign and Afghan contractors who are often corrupt. Unfortunately, the U.S. Department of Defense and allied ministries of defense have at best managed by exception when a few investigations have revealed gross negligence. They have never made proper planning and accountability key aspects of effective war fighting and transition.

The fiscal problems in the aid community get far more attention in spite of the fact that aid is a far smaller portion of the money that goes to corruption. Even so, the aid community reports largely in terms of plans, pledges, and commitments. The United Nations Assistance Mission in Afghanistan (UNAMA) has proven to be incompetent to the point of nearly total irresponsibility. It provides no meaningful reporting on the actual flow of aid or its effectiveness. It has never issued a meaningful report on the overall funding of aid activity in Afghanistan. The same is equally true of USAID [United States Agency for International Development] and the State Department, as well as most other foreign donor governments and NGOs. The reporting that does occur is largely in terms of money allocated or spent and projects started or completed. There is no meaningful reporting or transparency on the actual flow of money that reaches Afghans, no accountability, no meaning validation of project and program requirements, and no meaningful analysis of effectiveness.

Most Corrupt Countries in the World, 2012

1. Somalia
1. North Korea
1. Afghanistan
2. Sudan
3. Myanmar
4. Uzbekistan
4. Turkmenistan
5. Iraq
6. Haiti
6. Venezuela

TAKEN FROM: Simon Rogers, "Corruption Index 2012 from Transparency International: Find Out How Countries Compare," *Guardian*, December 5, 2012.

SIGAR concentrates its activities almost solely on U.S. military and civilian assistance. This major shortcoming has led to a near crippling lack of focus on overall Department of Defense and allied/donor spending. SIGAR estimates that total aid for civil projects and ANSF [Afghan National Security Forces] development from 2002 to 2010 has totaled some $62.1 billion—of which the US provided 81%, or $50.5 billion. Groups like Oxfam have put the wastage in aid spending at something like 40% of the total, but this includes overhead and security. No one really knows just how bad the situation is.

"Existentialist" Corruption

U.S. actions have exacerbated this lack of control over vast flows of funds to a country with a GDP [gross domestic product] of only $27 billion in 2009 and a per capita income of under $1,000:

> The U.S. played a key role in drafting a constitution that put virtually all money given to the Afghan government under

the control of the president and central government ministries that had little capacity to govern and no meaningful checks and balances.

The U.S. stood by as the Afghan civil service fell apart during the year after the U.S. drove out the Taliban. The few elements of government capacity Afghanistan had remaining left for other jobs or turned to corruption to survive.

The U.S. focused on Iraq through 2008 and spent more than twice as much on Iraq during this period as on Afghanistan. When it finally reacted to the rise of the insurgency, it put money into fighting the Taliban in the field and not into providing security for the Afghan people until the strategy changed in mid-2009.

The Congressional Research Service (CRS) reports that the U.S. budgeted some $428 billion for Department of Defense activity from FY 2001 to FY 2010, but only $25.2 billion for the U.S. State Department and USAID.

The U.S. never staffed an integrated system for controlling and evaluating contacts and expenditures or established proper audit and reporting procedures—in spite of repeated warnings by the U.S. Government Accountability Office (GAO) and the inspector general of the Department of Defense. This severely limited the ability of agency inspector generals to operate, and when SIGAR was finally established, its mission was limited, and it was not resourced to even moderate levels until 2009.

The U.S. never fully supported the High Office of Oversight (HOO), which should be the prime agency in the Afghan government for fighting corruption. Sources in the country team warn that the lack of genuine assistance reported in SIGAR's December 2009 report remains the same today.

The bulk of the money actually spent inside Afghanistan went through poorly supervised military contracts and through aid projects where the emphasis was speed, projected starts, and measuring progress in terms of spending rather than results. The U.S. stood by as contracting became a process in which U.S. and foreign contractors poured money into a limited number of Afghan power brokers who set up companies that were corrupt and did not perform. The U.S. also failed to properly ensure that the few power brokers caught in extreme corruption did not form new corporations. In many cases, they also paid off insurgents to let them operate.

Cargo movement in Afghanistan became a contract operation with private security forces. These cargo movement operations paid off the ANP [Afghan National Police], . . . and often insurgents—helping to create legal and illegal checkpoints along most Afghan roads.

The U.S. led an effort to create Afghan forces that took years to acquire meaningful resources and left key elements—especially the police—without adequate pay and with no real controls over how money was spent. When the U.S. finally assigned this a far higher priority, it set grossly overambitious goals that focus on quantity over quality and have massive shortfalls in U.S. and allied personnel. The U.S. and its allies could not manage the resulting contracting process. . . .

Worsening Problems

These problems became worse with time. The flow of money increased in direct proportion to the seriousness of the fighting, the expansion of Taliban control, and a steady decline in Afghan security. Moreover, the lack of effective and honest governance meant that no one could count on keeping a government job or the security of a business. Afghans had to do what they could to survive and this meant that all saw a steady rise in corruption and the role of power brokers at every level. The end result was that corruption became an "existential necessity" for those who could get the money while other Afghans fell into deeper poverty and a steadily less secure life.

Until the U.S. shifted to a population-centric strategy in late 2009, the Afghan people were left without effective governance and without any coherent attempt to give them security. They had every incentive to take what they could from a corrupt government while they could. Given government and military salaries, many officials, military personnel, and police officers had little choice. Corruption not only took place at the top—it became an "existentialist" necessity at mid-levels and the bottom.

These pressures were compounded by further U.S.-led failings and mistakes. The U.S. pushed for the eradication of narcotics in ways that made it remarkably easy for power brokers to keep making profits while using the eradication programs against their rivals. In the process, it pushed narcotics production into the hands of the Taliban and gave the enemy a major source of wealth. It also focused on a formal rule of law program so limited in scope and impact that the Afghan people were left with no source of prompt justice in many areas other than the Taliban, and the police had no functioning courts or jails. At the same time, the U.S. failed to seriously fund and staff the training of Afghan security forces until 2009. The police were so poorly paid and had so much authority that police corruption became a nightmare for many ordinary Afghans.

> *"The CIA and other foreign organizations certainly helped, but the final responsibility for corruption throughout Afghanistan rests with Afghans themselves."*

Afghan Officials Are Responsible for High Levels of Corruption in Afghanistan

Brian Cloughley

Brian Cloughley is a former soldier who writes on military and political affairs mainly concerning the subcontinent. He is the author of A History of the Pakistan Army: Wars and Insurrections. *In the following viewpoint, he argues that, while the United States and foreign donors have contributed to the problem, it is Afghans themselves who are ultimately responsible for the country's terrible corruption. Cloughley points in particular to Hamid Karzai, whom he says is a weak and ineffectual leader who has blatantly enriched himself through corruption. He also says that bribery is rampant throughout Afghanistan.*

As you read, consider the following questions:

   1. According to the viewpoint, who was Henry Brooke?

2. How did Karl Eikenberry describe Hamid Karzai?

3. According to Cloughley, what should Pakistan's policy be in Afghanistan?

During the Second [Anglo-]Afghan War (1878–1880) there was a particularly competent British army officer called Henry Brooke whose well-written diaries of the period are published as *Brigade Commander: Afghanistan*. He had little time for Afghans, and in April 1880 wrote that "an Afghan is so natural a liar that no one thinks of believing them, and among themselves they are never weak enough to put any trust one in the other, and in this they are quite wise as a more treacherous set of lying beings do not, I suppose, exist on the face of the world."

The Most Corrupt Country

Of course it is not politically correct in this enlightened age to heed the words of an imperialist creature of a British Raj [British rule in the Indian subcontinent] that was intent on crushing innocent people who were living lives of moral cloudlessness, agreeable democracy and social tranquility before being subjected to the attentions of the dreaded colonialists. But in spite of that, you do have to admit that Brooke had a point—and that perhaps his point remains relevant today. And he could have added some words about corruption to his observations.

Along with North Korea and Somalia, Afghanistan is the world's most corrupt country, and some of its most influential citizens have worked hard to achieve that deplorable ranking.

Certainly there is much sleaze elsewhere—in Pakistan, for example, which is 37th in the world dishonesty list. India's standing is less awful, but its rip-off quotient is majestically greater, with, for example, the Commonwealth Games in Delhi in 2010 having involved embezzlement of over a billion dollars, according to the current *New Yorker*.

None of this can be excused, of course, but in Afghanistan corruption has achieved an art form and is probably one of the gravest problems the country has to face. It starts right at the top. In April [2013], the *New York Times* reported that, "For more than a decade, wads of American dollars packed into suitcases, backpacks and, on occasion, plastic shopping bags have been dropped off every month or so at the offices of Afghanistan's president—courtesy of the Central Intelligence Agency [CIA]. All told, tens of millions of dollars have flowed from the CIA to the office of President Hamid Karzai. . . . An American official said, 'The biggest source of corruption in Afghanistan [is] the United States.'"

Now that's pretty blunt, but perhaps just this once the US is not entirely to blame for the shambles in a country it invaded. The CIA and other foreign organizations certainly helped, but the final responsibility for corruption throughout Afghanistan rests with Afghans themselves.

Swamped in Sleaze

The head of the UN's [United Nations'] Office on Drugs and Crime, Jean-Luc Lemahieu, said in February that "the bribes that Afghan citizens paid in 2012 equal double Afghanistan's domestic revenue." This revelation attracted no condemnatory reaction from President Karzai or any other influential Afghan, which is not surprising because he and many members of his government and officialdom are the main benefactors from the sleaze that swamps their country.

Karzai's character was well described by US Ambassador Karl Eikenberry in a leaked cable in which he wrote of "a paranoid and weak individual unfamiliar with the basics of nation-building." That sums him up very well. His posturing on the world stage has been as unimpressive as it has been counterproductive—and his August visit to Pakistan was both.

Afterwards, Karzai said he had asked Pakistan Prime Minister Nawaz Sharif to provide a platform for talks between the

Afghan High Peace Council and the Taliban. But of course he well knows that Pakistan has been trying for years to facilitate dialogue. (As do the Americans who so vociferously blame Pakistan for allegedly failing to do anything to help resolve the chaos caused by their amateur dabbling in that admittedly bewildering country.)

Yet Kabul has itself imposed a block on the way to improving relations with Islamabad, illustrated by Karzai earlier this year when he declared that, "Since the Durand line [international border] has been imposed on Afghanistan, it was not acceptable to the Afghans and we cannot accept the Durand line."   •

The Failings of Karzai

This is patently nonsense and entirely counterproductive. The border has been acknowledged by Afghanistan for many years—except when convenient to flap red herrings in the way of progress to dialogue. Karzai is well-deserving of Eikenberry's observations that he lacks the ability "to grasp the most rudimentary principles of state-building" and that given his "reputation for shady dealings, his recommendations for large, costly infrastructure projects should be viewed with a healthy dose of skepticism."

Barely believably, Hamid Karzai holds a major British Order of Chivalry, having accepted appointment as an honorary Knight Grand Cross of the Order of St Michael and St George in 2003. (On occasions Her Majesty the Queen has to appoint some pretty queer fish to such eminence on the "advice" of the prime minister of the day, who at Karzai's knight time was the egregious Tony Blair.)

It is strange that the president of the Islamic Republic of Afghanistan should accept an honor that commemorates two Christian holy men, but perhaps it serves to highlight the fact that he is himself no saint. He has not served his country well in the chaotic years of his presidency, and his endorsement of corruption will have disastrous effects for long after he has departed.

Unfortunately, so, too, will his legacy of general incompetence and hostility to Pakistan—the only country that Afghanistan can rely on in the long term. There are lots of pieces to be picked up in Afghanistan, but Pakistan should stay on the sidelines for the moment, quietly continuing contact with all parties and waiting for a more balanced and competent leader in Kabul. And always bearing in mind the opinion (which might be exaggerated, of course) that "an Afghan is so natural a liar that no one thinks of believing them. . . ."

> *"There are areas where you need strong leadership, and some of those leaders are not entirely pure.... But they can help us be more effective in going after the primary threat, which is the Taliban."*

U.S. to Temper Stance on Afghan Corruption

Greg Jaffe

Greg Jaffe is a writer for the Washington Post. *In the following viewpoint, he reports that US military officials have decided that they need to accept a certain amount of corruption to focus on the fight against the Taliban. Efforts to reduce corruption will continue, Jaffe says, but in some cases the United States will work with corrupt officials because removing them would create a power vacuum that the Taliban could exploit.*

As you read, consider the following questions:

1. What incident does Jaffe say has given the question of corruption a new urgency?

2. How did the United States deal with corruption linked to Hamid Karzai's brother Ahmed Wali Karzai?

3. According to Lt. Gen. David Rodriguez, why are representative local councils important to US strategy?

U.S. commanders in southern Afghanistan are adopting a strategy that increasingly places the priority on fighting the Taliban even if that means tolerating some corruption.

Anti-Corruption Could Be Destabilizing

Military officials in the region have concluded that the Taliban's insurgency is the most pressing threat to stability in some areas and that a sweeping effort to drive out corruption could create chaos and a governance vacuum that the Taliban could exploit.

"There are areas where you need strong leadership, and some of those leaders are not entirely pure," said a senior defense official. "But they can help us be more effective in going after the primary threat, which is the Taliban."

The issue of corruption in Afghanistan has taken on renewed urgency in recent weeks with the arrest of a senior aide to President Hamid Karzai and new questions about Kabul's commitment to fighting graft. Senior [Barack] Obama administration officials have repeatedly emphasized the need to root out graft in Afghanistan and have deployed teams of FBI [Federal Bureau of Investigation] and Drug Enforcement Administration agents to assemble corruption cases. The United States has spent about $50 billion to promote reconstruction in Afghanistan since 2001.

It was not immediately clear whether the White House, the State Department and law enforcement agencies share the military's views, which come at a critical time for U.S. forces in Afghanistan. After an eight-month buildup, the 30,000 additional soldiers and Marines that President Obama ordered to this country are almost entirely in place, allowing U.S. and

Afghan forces to conduct sweeps of Taliban strongholds and detain insurgent leaders at the highest levels of the nearly nine-year-long war, military officials said.

Defense Secretary Robert M. Gates visited two U.S. Army units on Friday that had been hit with tough losses in recent days as they cleared insurgents from areas in and around this southern Afghanistan city, the spiritual home of the Taliban and the site of some of the heaviest fighting for U.S. and Afghan forces.

"It has been a tough week for you," Gates told soldiers from an Army battalion that had lost seven soldiers this week. "Unfortunately, there are going to be more tough weeks ahead."

Kandahar Campaign

The Kandahar campaign reflects the breadth of the problems that the United States faces throughout Afghanistan and explains why some U.S. officials are reluctant to take too hard a line on Afghan corruption. "Kandahar is not just a Taliban problem; it is a mafia, criminal syndicate problem," the senior defense official said, speaking on the condition of anonymity because of the sensitivity of the subject. "That is why it is so complicated. But clearly the most pressing threat is the Taliban."

Some military and civilian advisers to the U.S.-led command in Kabul argue for a comprehensive effort to root out graft and other official abuses, contending that government corruption and ineffectiveness have prompted many Afghans to support the insurgency. "You can't separate the fight against corruption from the fight against the Taliban," one of the advisers said. "They are intimately linked."

But U.S. officials and defense analysts say that challenging local power brokers and criminal syndicates, many of which depend on U.S. reconstruction contracts and ties to the Afghan government for support, would likely add to the unrest

Kabul Bank Scandal

The Kabul Bank scandal has perhaps been the most visible and damaging case of corruption to date in Afghanistan. Prior to the scandal, Kabul Bank held accounts for several key ministries and paid the salaries for civil servants, teachers, police and other government employees. It is reported that the bank's management had ties to key power holders including Vice President Marshal Fahim and the brother of the president, Mahmoud Karzai, who allegedly received a significant loan from the Kabul Bank to buy his share in the bank. In September 2010, when hundreds of millions of dollars in losses were reported, primarily from shareholder investments in Dubai, there was effectively a run on the bank. Public confidence in the banking system was severely eroded. The International Monetary Fund (IMF) suspended its credit programme to the Afghan government, requesting an audit of Afghan banks, and several donors (including the UK [United Kingdom]) suspended, but have since resumed, funding to the Afghanistan Reconstruction Trust Fund.

International Development Committee
of the British House of Commons, "Afghanistan:
Development Progress and Prospects After 2014," 2012, p. 13.

in southern Afghanistan and produce a higher U.S. casualty rate. "Putting an end to these patronage networks would not come cheaply," said Stephen Biddle, a senior fellow at the Council on Foreign Relations who has advised U.S. commanders in Afghanistan.

By contrast, allowing some graft among Afghan power brokers on the condition that they agree to limit their take and moderate predatory activities, such as their use of illegal police checkpoints, could promote near-term improvements, Biddle said. "We spend a lot more money in Afghanistan than the narcotics trade," he said. "A lot of money that funds these networks comes from us. So we can essentially de-fund these networks, taking away their contracts."

The military's strategy on corruption appears to more broadly apply conclusions reached earlier this year by top military officers in Kandahar. Some diplomats and military officers had recommended the removal of Karzai's brother, Ahmed Wali Karzai, as the chairman of the Kandahar province council, but Gen. Stanley A. McChrystal, the top U.S. commander in Afghanistan at the time, eventually concluded that there was no clear evidence of wrongdoing and that ousting him could leave a power vacuum in the area.

Instead, the military has sought to limit the amount of money flowing to Ahmed Wali Karzai by awarding lucrative contracts for supplies and services to firms that he and his relatives do not control.

Recently, Gen. David H. Petraeus, the top commander in Afghanistan, asked a group of senior officers to study more closely how U.S. reconstruction and logistics contracts are awarded. He also said he planned to publish contracting rules that would help ensure that U.S. spending practices weren't fueling discontent by excluding influential groups and driving them to support the Taliban insurgency. Such a move would be welcomed by President Karzai, who has argued that foreign money is fueling corruption.

Gates also has said that the United States must do more to ensure that its contracting practices aren't fueling corruption.

Local Councils

The growing understanding that military commanders will have to work with some corrupt officials and warlords hasn't led them to abandon time-consuming efforts to build local government capacity. In areas where U.S. and Afghan forces have driven out the Taliban, they are working with locals to assemble councils made up of elders that will help decide how reconstruction money is spent and serve as a check on government abuses.

"That representative council is important because that is really the link between the people and the district leadership," said Lt. Gen. David Rodriguez, the second-ranking U.S. commander in Afghanistan.

Even building effective local councils will take time in areas where U.S. forces have little to no knowledge of the key players and power relationships.

U.S. forces are only now beginning to push into areas that have had little or no American presence in recent years and to develop an intimate knowledge of the players and power relationships.

"We have never had the granular understanding of local circumstances in Afghanistan that we achieved over time in Iraq," Petraeus said this week. "One of the key elements in our ability to be fairly agile in our activities in Iraq during the surge was a pretty good understanding of who the power brokers were in local areas and how the systems were supposed to work and how they really worked. . . . That enabled us enormously."

"Corruption is endemic; woven into the very fabric of society and in particular public institutions."

Taliban Preys on Afghanistan's Corrupt Police Force

Brian Brady

Brian Brady is Whitehall editor for the Independent on Sunday. *In the following viewpoint, he reports on ongoing issues of corruption in the Afghan police force. He writes that the Afghan police have serious problems with drug addiction and that the force is hated and feared for its practices of extortion and illegal taxation. He says that the corruption will not be much improved by the time British forces leave in 2014 and that it will have a serious effect on efforts to increase confidence in government and defeat the Taliban.*

As you read, consider the following questions:

1. What does Hamid Karzai claim is the source of corruption in Afghanistan?

2. What steps did a report on the Afghan Uniform Police (AUP) in Helmand province recommend to reduce corruption?

3. What is the illiteracy rate among Afghan National Police (ANP) troops, and what is the rate of drug use?

The Afghan police charged with maintaining security in their own country as coalition troops begin to pull out within months are still "endemically corrupt" and riven with problems including nepotism and drug abuse, internal government documents have revealed.

Foreign and Commonwealth Office (FCO) papers obtained by the *Independent on Sunday* disclose official concerns about the fate of Afghanistan and its chances of holding the Taliban at bay, if its leaders fail to "root out corruption" throughout the ranks of the Afghan National Police (ANP).

A confidential report on the performance of the Afghan Uniform Police (AUP), the nation's major law enforcement body, observed in October: "Unless radical change is introduced to improve the actual and perceived integrity and legitimacy of officers within the AUP, then the organisation will continue to provide an ineffective and tainted service to citizens . . . for decades to come."

The assessments, in a series of official FCO documents, lay bare the continuing anxieties over the war-torn country's capacity to function as a democratic state when international troops begin withdrawing from their combat role in the country in 2013. The vast majority are scheduled to be out by the end of 2014.

The details come only days after David Cameron said during a visit to Afghanistan that British troops could be withdrawn even more quickly than planned, because local security forces were "doing better than expected". The prime minister announced that UK numbers would be nearly halved to 5,200 next year, as part of the withdrawal plan.

The Afghan president, Hamid Karzai, yesterday accepted that widespread corruption was "a bitter reality" but claimed it was largely fuelled by the countries funding his government and security forces.

"The part of this corruption that is in our offices is a small part: that is bribes," the president said in a speech on national television. "The other part of corruption, the large part, is hundreds of millions of dollars that are not ours. We shouldn't blame ourselves for that. That part is from others and imposed on us."

However, the FCO reports a catalogue of homegrown problems with Afghanistan's police, which could hinder the country's development in future years.

In October, a report on the AUP in Helmand province questioned the chances of achieving the police's stated goal of "eliminating corruption all over the country".

The report observed: "Whilst this is undeniably a laudable aspiration, the reality of the situation in Afghanistan is that corruption is endemic; woven into the very fabric of society and in particular public institutions. This fact renders the objective unachievable, with some commentators arguing that the issue is generational and cannot therefore be dealt with effectively for many years to come."

The report called for a complaints procedure and action against "patronage and nepotism issues in the appointment of senior officers".

It added: "The continued absence of a reliable system for recruiting and promoting AUP officers will see the status quo being maintained, where people motivated by personal gain and/or harbouring nefarious intent have access to senior and influential roles within the service."

Another FCO paper . . . stated that the justice sector was improving, but it added: "Anti-corruption efforts are off-track, with political interference notable in high-level prosecutions."

ANP officers, who are usually at the front line of the security forces' dealings with the public, have to endure lower pay and fatality rates twice as high as their counterparts in the Afghan army. But one paper, entitled "Changes in ANP", observed that: "The Afghan police suffer from many problems.

Of the 82,000 nominally serving on the force, around 60,000 are believed to be working. We estimate over 70 per cent are illiterate, and drug abuse is an issue."

The rate of drug use among ANP officers was estimated at 9 per cent, compared to a national average of 8 per cent.

Another report, assessing the ANP's progress, reported that the force had "shortcomings in a number of areas", including corruption and theft. It added: "Concerns remain about corruption, criminal activity, drug use and the lack of a clear 'end state' for the force. The ANP is viewed negatively by the population, with multiple reports of illegal taxation, extortion and other serious crimes, as well as drug addiction."

The Labour MP Sandra Osborne, a member of the Defence Select Committee, said the Afghan police were "hated". She added: "It will take years for a fully legitimate police force to come about, if ever. Eventually it will be up to the Afghan government, and that is the real problem, as is widely recognised the lack of a stable political settlement."

Roland Paris, director of the Centre for International Policy Studies at the University of Ottawa, said: "Prime Minister Cameron is declaring success prematurely. There is little reason to believe that the ANP will be significantly more effective or less corrupt in 2014."

An FCO spokeswoman said the development of Afghan National Security Forces (ANSF) was "a significant achievement". She added: "It is because of the increasing strength, confidence and capability of the ANSF that the transition process is gaining momentum. As a result, UK forces will be able to move from mentoring at battalion level to brigade level by the end of 2013, thereby allowing a significant troop drawdown, as announced by the Prime Minister this week."

Periodical and Internet Sources Bibliography

The following articles have been selected to supplement the diverse views presented in this chapter.

Associated Press	"Afghanistan's Media Flourish in Taliban's Wake," CBS News, February 4, 2014.
Daily Times (Pakistan)	"Targeting Afghan Elections," March 25, 2014.
Heath Druzin	"Afghanistan Again at Bottom of Corruption Index," *Stars and Stripes*, December 3, 2013.
Kathy Gannon	"In Afghan Race, Wooing Votes with Ethnic Strongmen," Associated Press, March 24, 2014.
Eline Gordts	"U.S. Lacks Comprehensive Anti-Corruption Strategy in Afghanistan, Despite Sending Billions in Aid," *Huffington Post*, September 11, 2013.
Emma Graham-Harrison	"Afghanistan Election Guide: Everything You Need to Know," *Guardian*, February 3, 2014.
Jean MacKenzie	"Just How Corrupt Is Afghanistan?," GlobalPost, December 9, 2013.
Paul D. Shinkman	"Corruption Plagues Afghanistan Ahead of U.S. Withdrawal," *U.S. News & World Report*, December 27, 2013.
Jaswant Singh	"No Easy Route to Democracy," *Arab News*, March 22, 2014.
Thomas Sowell	"Another Galling Betrayal," Townhall.com, February 18, 2014.
Jeffrey E. Stern	"Afghanistan's Growing Identity (Card) Crisis," *Foreign Policy*, January 21, 2014.
Alicia P.Q. Wittmeyer	"When No One's Looking," *Foreign Policy*, March 12, 2014.

OPPOSING
VIEWPOINTS®
SERIES

CHAPTER 3

What Are Economic Issues in Afghanistan?

Chapter Preface

One of the most devastating signs of the failure of Afghanistan's economy is widespread child malnutrition. In a September 4, 2012, article at the *Guardian*, Emma Graham-Harrison reported that despite large-scale foreign aid donation, "a third of young children in southern Afghanistan are acutely malnourished, with a level of deprivation similar to that found in famine zones."

The problem in Afghanistan is not food itself; there is no shortage. Rather, nutritional problems are caused by poverty, lack of basic nutritional knowledge, and health care. Many families do not breast-feed or have trouble breast-feeding and do not have funds to pay for adequate alternatives, relying instead on water or tea or over-diluted formula. Getting to doctors or hospitals can be difficult or impossible given poor infrastructure and family poverty.

Since 2012, when Graham-Harrison wrote her initial account, the situation has not improved. If anything, it has gotten worse, according to Rod Nordland, writing in a January 4, 2014, article in the *New York Times*. In 2014 severe malnutrition among children had increased by 50 percent from the already dismal levels of 2012. The cause of the intensifying hunger crisis is difficult to pin down, but it seems linked to the war. Malnutrition is especially bad in provinces like Kandahar and Farah, which have seen heavy fighting. But even in the capital of Kabul, the situation is worsening. As Nordland says,

> Nearly every potential lifeline is strained or broken here. Efforts to educate people about nutrition and health care are often stymied by conservative traditions that cloister women away from anyone outside the family. Agriculture and traditional local sources of social support have been disrupted by war and the widespread flight of refugees to the cities. And therapeutic feeding programs, complex operations even in

countries with strong health care systems, have been compromised as the flow of aid and transportation have been derailed by political tensions or violence.

In this, as in so many ways, Afghanistan's improving economy and the welfare of its people are stymied by the unending conflict.

The authors in the following chapter examine other economic issues in Afghanistan, including the country's opium crop and mineral resources.

"*The war on Afghanistan is part of a profit-driven agenda: a war of economic conquest and plunder, 'a resource war.'*"

The Afghan War Is Driven by Desire for Afghanistan's Mineral Resources

Michel Chossudovsky

Michel Chossudovsky is professor emeritus of economics at the University of Ottawa and the author of America's "War on Terrorism." *In the following viewpoint, he argues that Afghanistan has vast mineral and gas resources, and that, contrary to recent news reporting, the United States has known about these assets for a long time. Chossudovsky argues that the 2001 US invasion of Afghanistan was not done to combat terrorism but rather was an imperial effort to obtain control of the country's resources.*

As you read, consider the following questions:

1. Why is lithium an increasingly vital resource, according to the author?

2. What precious stones are found in Afghanistan's pegmatite fields to the east of Kabul, according to Chossudovsky?

3. How much money does Chossudovsky say the drug trade in Afghanistan currently generates?

The 2001 bombing and invasion of Afghanistan has been presented to world public opinion as a "Just War," a war directed against the Taliban and al Qaeda, a war to eliminate "Islamic terrorism" and instate Western-style democracy.

Real Objectives

The economic dimensions of the "Global War on Terrorism" (GWOT) are rarely mentioned. The post 9/11 "counter-terrorism campaign" has served to obfuscate the real objectives of the US-NATO [North Atlantic Treaty Organization] war.

The war on Afghanistan is part of a profit-driven agenda: a war of economic conquest and plunder, "a resource war."

While Afghanistan is acknowledged as a strategic hub in central Asia, bordering on the former Soviet Union, China and Iran, at the crossroads of pipeline routes and major oil and gas reserves, its huge mineral wealth as well as its untapped natural gas reserves have remained, until June 2010, totally unknown to the American public.

According to a joint report by the Pentagon, the US Geological Survey (USGS) and USAID [United States Agency for International Development], Afghanistan is now said to possess "previously unknown" and untapped mineral reserves, estimated authoritatively to be of the order of one trillion dollars. (*New York Times*, U.S. Identifies Vast Mineral Riches in Afghanistan—NYTimes.com, June 14, 2010. See also BBC, 14 June 2010).

The previously unknown deposits—including huge veins of iron, copper, cobalt, gold and critical industrial metals like lithium—are so big and include so many minerals that are essential to modern industry that Afghanistan could eventually be transformed into one of the most important mining centers in the world, the United States officials believe.

An internal Pentagon memo, for example, states that Afghanistan could become the "Saudi Arabia of lithium," a key raw material in the manufacture of batteries for laptops and BlackBerrys.

The vast scale of Afghanistan's mineral wealth was discovered by a small team of Pentagon officials and American geologists. The Afghan government and President Hamid Karzai were recently briefed, American officials said.

While it could take many years to develop a mining industry, the potential is so great that officials and executives in the industry believe it could attract heavy investment even before mines are profitable, providing the possibility of jobs that could distract from generations of war.

"There is stunning potential here," Gen. David H. Petraeus, commander of the United States Central Command, said. "There are a lot of ifs, of course, but I think potentially it is hugely significant."

The value of the newly discovered mineral deposits dwarfs the size of Afghanistan's existing war-bedraggled economy, which is based largely on opium production and narcotics trafficking as well as aid from the United States and other industrialized countries. Afghanistan's gross domestic product is only about $12 billion.

"This will become the backbone of the Afghan economy," said Jalil Jumriany, an adviser to the Afghan minister of mines. (*New York Times*, op cit).

Afghanistan could become, according to the *New York Times* "the Saudi Arabia of lithium." "Lithium is an increasingly vital resource, used in batteries for everything from mobile phones to laptops and key to the future of the electric car." At present Chile, Australia, China and Argentina are the main suppliers of lithium to the world market. Bolivia and Chile are the countries with the largest known reserves of lithium. The Pentagon has been conducting ground surveys in western Afghanistan. "Pentagon officials said that their initial analysis at one location in Ghazni province showed the potential for lithium deposits as large as those of Bolivia." (U.S. Identifies Vast Mineral Riches in Afghanistan—NYTimes.com, June 14, 2010, see also Lithium—Wikipedia, the free encyclopedia).

"Previously Unknown Deposits" of Minerals in Afghanistan

The Pentagon's near one trillion dollar "estimate" of previously "unknown deposits" is a useful smokescreen. The Pentagon's one trillion dollar figure is more a trumped up number rather than an estimate: "We took a look at what we knew to be there, and asked what would it be worth now in terms of today's dollars. *The trillion dollar figure seemed to be newsworthy.*" (*The Sunday Times*, London, June 15 2010, emphasis added).

Moreover, the results of a US Geological Survey study (quoted in the Pentagon memo) on Afghanistan's mineral wealth were revealed three years back, at a 2007 conference organized by the Afghan-American Chamber of Commerce. The matter of Afghanistan's mineral riches, however, was not considered newsworthy at the time.

The US administration's acknowledgment that it first took cognizance of Afghanistan's vast mineral wealth following the release of the USGS 2007 report is an obvious red herring. Afghanistan's mineral wealth and energy resources (including natural gas) were known to both America's business elites and the US government prior to the Soviet-Afghan war (1979–1988).

Geological surveys conducted by the Soviet Union in the 1970s and early 1980s confirm the existence of vast reserves of copper (among the largest in Eurasia), iron, high-grade chrome ore, uranium, beryl, barite, lead, zinc, fluorspar, bauxite, lithium, tantalum, emeralds, gold and silver. (Afghanistan, Mining Annual Review, *The Mining Journal*, June 1984). These surveys suggest that the actual value of these reserves could indeed be substantially larger than the one trillion dollars "estimate" intimated by the Pentagon-USGS-USAID study.

More recently, in a 2002 report, the Kremlin confirmed what was already known: "It's no secret that Afghanistan possesses rich reserves, in particular of copper at the Aynak deposit, iron ore, . . . uranium, polymetallic ore, oil and gas," (RIA Novosti, January 6, 2002).

Afghanistan has never been anyone's colony—no foreigner had ever "dug" here before the 1950s. The Hindu Kush mountains, stretching, together with their foothills, over a vast area in Afghanistan, are where the minerals lie. Over the past 40 years, several dozen deposits have been discovered in Afghanistan, and most of these discoveries were sensational. They were kept secret, however, but even so certain facts have recently become known.

It turns out that Afghanistan possesses reserves of nonferrous and ferrous metals and precious stones, and, if exploited, they would possibly be able to cover even the earnings from the drug industry. The copper deposit in Aynak in the southern Afghan Helmand province is said to be the largest in the Eurasian continent, and its location (40 km from Kabul) makes it cheap to develop. The iron ore deposit at Hajigak in the central Bamyan province yields ore of an extraordinarily high quality, the reserves of which are estimated to be 500m tonnes. A coal deposit has also been discovered not far from there.

Afghanistan is spoken of as a transit country for oil and gas. However, only a very few people know that Soviet specialists discovered huge gas reserves there in the 1960s and built the first gas pipeline in the country to supply gas to Uzbekistan. At that time, the Soviet Union used to receive 2.5 bn cubic metres of Afghan gas annually. During the same period, large deposits of gold, fluorite, barytes and marble onyxes that have a very rare pattern were found.

However, the pegmatite fields discovered to the east of Kabul are a real sensation. Rubies, beryllium, emeralds and kunzites and hiddenites that cannot be found anywhere else—the deposits of these precious stones stretch for hundreds of kilometres. Also, the rocks containing the rare metals beryllium, thorium, lithium and tantalum are of strategic importance (they are used in air and spacecraft construction)....

While public opinion was fed images of a war-torn resourceless developing country, the realities are otherwise: Afghanistan is a rich country as confirmed by Soviet-era geological surveys.

The issue of "previously unknown deposits" sustains a falsehood. It excludes Afghanstan's vast mineral wealth as a justifiable *casus belli*. It says that the Pentagon only recently became aware that Afghanistan was among the world's most wealthy mineral economies, comparable to the Democratic Republic of the Congo, or former Zaire of the Mobutu [Sese Seko] era. The Soviet geopolitical reports were known. During the Cold War, all this information was known in minute detail.

Extensive Soviet exploration produced superb geological maps and reports that listed more than 1,400 mineral outcroppings, along with about 70 commercially viable deposits.... The Soviet Union subsequently committed more than $650 million for resource exploration and development in Afghanistan, with proposed projects including an oil refinery capable of producing a half-million tons per annum, as well as a smelting complex for the Aynak deposit that was to have produced 1.5 million tons of copper per year. In the wake of the Soviet withdrawal a subsequent World Bank analysis projected that the Aynak copper production alone could eventually capture as much as 2 percent of the annual world market. The country is also blessed with massive coal deposits, one of which, the Hajigak iron deposit, in the Hindu Kush mountain range west of Kabul, is assessed as one of the largest

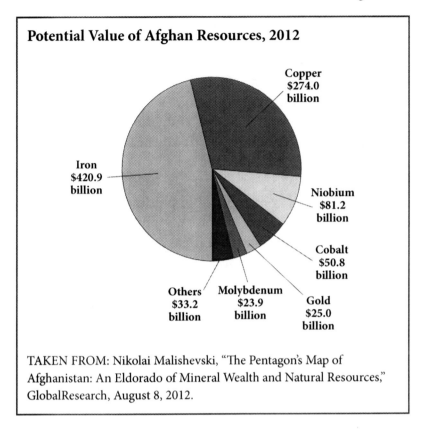

Potential Value of Afghan Resources, 2012

Copper $274.0 billion

Iron $420.9 billion

Niobium $81.2 billion

Cobalt $50.8 billion

Others $33.2 billion

Molybdenum $23.9 billion

Gold $25.0 billion

TAKEN FROM: Nikolai Malishevski, "The Pentagon's Map of Afghanistan: An Eldorado of Mineral Wealth and Natural Resources," GlobalResearch, August 8, 2012.

high-grade deposits in the world. (John C.K. Daly, Analysis: Afghanistan's Untapped Energy Riches, UPI, October 24, 2008).

Afghanistan's Natural Gas

Afghanistan is a land bridge. The 2001 U.S.-led invasion and occupation of Afghanistan has been analysed by critics of US foreign policy as a means to securing control over the strategic trans-Afghan transport corridor which links the Caspian Sea basin to the Arabian sea.

Several trans-Afghan oil and gas pipeline projects have been contemplated including the planned $8.0 billion TAPI pipeline project (Turkmenistan, Afghanistan, Pakistan, India) of 1900 km, which would transport Turkmen natural gas across Afghanistan in what is described as a "crucial transit corridor." (See Gary Olson, Afghanistan Has Never Been the 'Good and Necessary' War; It's About Control of Oil, The Morning Call, October 1, 2009). Military escalation under the extended Af-Pak [Afghanistan and Pakistan] war bears a relationship to TAPI. Turkmenistan possesses the third largest natural gas reserves after Russia and Iran. Strategic control over the transport routes out of Turkmenistan have been part of Washington's agenda since the collapse of the Soviet Union in 1991.

What was rarely contemplated in pipeline geopolitics, however, is that Afghanistan is not only adjacent to countries which are rich in oil and natural gas (e.g., Turkmenistan), it also possesses within its territory sizeable untapped reserves of natural gas, coal and oil. Soviet estimates of the 1970s placed "Afghanistan's 'explored' (proved plus probable) gas reserves at about 5 trillion cubic feet. The Hodja-Gugerdag's initial reserves were placed at slightly more than 2 tcf." (*See, The Soviet Union to Retain Influence in Afghanistan, Oil & Gas Journal, May 2, 1988*).

The US Energy Information Administration (EIA) acknowledged in 2008 that Afghanistan's natural gas reserves are "substantial":

"As northern Afghanistan is a 'southward extension of central Asia's highly prolific, natural gas-prone Amu Darya basin,' Afghanistan 'has proven, probable and possible natural gas reserves of about 5 trillion cubic feet.'" (John C.K. Daly, Analysis: Afghanistan's Untapped Energy Riches, UPI, October 24, 2008).

From the outset of the Soviet-Afghan war in 1979, Washington's objective has been to sustain a geopolitical foothold in central Asia.

The Golden Crescent Drug Trade

America's covert war, namely its support to the Mujahideen "freedom fighters" (aka [terrorist group] al Qaeda) was also geared towards the development of the Golden Crescent trade in opiates, which was used by US intelligence to fund the insurgency directed against the Soviets.

Instated at the outset of the Soviet-Afghan war and protected by the CIA [Central Intelligence Agency], the drug trade developed over the years into a highly lucrative multibillion-dollar undertaking. It was the cornerstone of America's covert war in the 1980s. Today, under US-NATO [North Atlantic Treaty Organization] military occupation, the drug trade generates cash earnings in Western markets in excess of $200 billion dollars a year. (See Michel Chossudovsky, America's War on Terrorism, Global Research, Montreal, 2005; see also Michel Chossudovsky, Heroin Is "Good for Your Health": Occupation Forces Support Afghan Narcotics Trade, Global Research, April 29, 2007).

Towards an Economy of Plunder

The US media, in chorus, has upheld the "recent discovery" of Afghanistan's mineral wealth as "a solution" to the development of the country's war-torn economy as well as a means to eliminating poverty. The 2001 US-NATO invasion and occupation has set the stage for their appropriation by Western mining and energy conglomerates.

The war on Afghanistan is a profit-driven "resource war."

Under US and allied occupation, this mineral wealth is slated to be plundered, once the country has been pacified, by a handful of multinational mining conglomerates. According to Olga Borisova, writing in the months following the October 2001 invasion, the US-led "war on terrorism [will be transformed] into a colonial policy of influencing a fabulously wealthy country." (Borisova, op cit).

Part of the US-NATO agenda is also to eventually take possession of Afghanistan's reserves of natural gas, as well as prevent the development of competing Russian, Iranian and Chinese energy interests in Afghanistan.

"The resource argument seems to have been presented by the Pentagon when it was advantageous."

The Afghan War Is Not Driven by Desire for Resources

Daily Bell

The Daily Bell is a website that focuses on economics, politics, and free markets. The following viewpoint argues that the war in Afghanistan is not being fought for resources, though the Pentagon seems to want people to think that resources are an important reason for war in the country. The author maintains that fighting terrorism is not a convincing reason for the war either. Rather, the author concludes, the war is being fought to control Afghanistan and graft Western financial institutions onto the country. This goal is, however, failing.

As you read, consider the following questions:

1. What does the Daily Bell say are the three explanations for the war advanced in the alternative media?

2. According to *Foreign Policy*, why are the Pentagon's revelations about Afghan resource wealth suspicious?

3. Why is the West interested in Afghan Pashtuns and Pakistan Punjabis, according to the Daily Bell?

> Report brands Kabul Bank a fraud . . . Kabul Bank, which accounted for more than a third of Afghanistan's banking assets before it was seized by the authorities two years ago, was a billion-dollar fraud for the benefit of a few well-connected Afghans, says a report. "Its failure and subsequent bailout represents approximately 5–6 per cent of Afghanistan's gross domestic product, making Kabul Bank one of the largest banking failures in the world," stated Wednesday's report, funded by foreign donors, from the Independent Joint Anti-Corruption Monitoring and Evaluation Committee. "Every citizen in Afghanistan will bear the cost of the hundreds of millions of dollars required to secure deposits and the tens of millions of dollars required to deal with the aftermath," it said.—*Financial Times*

Dominant Social Theme: We will give Afghanistan Western tools and they will prosper with them.

Free-Market Analysis: The collapse of Kabul Bank can certainly be seen as a metaphor for the larger Afghan War. The idea was always to inflict Western-style regulatory democracy on Afghanistan. This seems ever clearer in hindsight.

Reasons for War

This is an important issue given the difference of opinion within the alternative media about the reasons for such wars. The justifications advanced within the alternative media context are three:

The first one is that such wars are resource wars, led by multinational corporations. The second is that such wars are prosecuted merely for the sake of their continuance. The military-industrial complex needs an "endless war." The third perspective, the one we have adopted, is that these are wars for control.

Of course, there are other reasons advanced as well for the current war on Afghanistan. These are mainstream media rationale and include the idea that NATO [North Atlantic Treaty Organization] needs to battle the [militant Islamic] Taliban to ensure that it doesn't take over Afghanistan again and that [terrorist group] al Qaeda doesn't return.

But the Taliban was put out of power ten years ago and al Qaeda is said to number only 100 or so fighting individuals in the whole of Afghanistan. It doesn't make much sense that the US and NATO have spent US$1 trillion or more and committed hundreds of thousands of dollars to fighting a war to hunt down a defeated enemy and eradicate 100 or so individuals.

The resource argument proves troublesome as well, in our view. It was announced in 2010 by the Pentagon that Afghanistan had US$1 trillion in resources. But an article in *Foreign Policy* entitled, "Say What? Afghanistan Has $1 Trillion in Untapped Mineral Resources?" states what we also believed at the time, that the announcement was political and aimed at shoring up a consensus for continuing the war.

In other words, the announcement about Afghanistan's mineral wealth was manufactured. The *Foreign Policy* writer put it this way:

> There's less to this scoop than meets the eye. For one thing, the findings on which the story was based are online and have been since 2007, courtesy of the U.S. Geological Survey [USGS]. More information is available on the Afghan mining ministry's website, including a report by the British Geological Survey (and there's more here). You can also take a look at the USGS's documentation of the airborne part of the survey here, including the full set of aerial photographs.
>
> Nowhere have I found that $1 trillion figure mentioned, which [writer James] Risen suggests was generated by a Pen-

tagon task force seeking to help the Afghan government develop its resources (looking at the chart accompanying the
article, though, it appears to be a straightforward tabulation
of the total reserve figures for each mineral times the current market price). According to Risen, that task force has
begun prepping the mining ministry to start soliciting bids
for mineral rights in the fall . . .

I'm (a) skeptical of that $1 trillion figure; (b) skeptical of
the timing of this story, given the bad news cycle, and (c)
skeptical that Afghanistan can really figure out a way to develop these resources in a useful way. It's also worth noting,
as Risen does, that it will take years to get any of this stuff
out of the ground, not to mention enormous capital investment.

War for Control

The resource argument seems to have been presented by the
Pentagon when it was advantageous. It was provided to justify
the war, which is exactly what makes us suspicious of it. Critics of the war can continue to make the case that rapacious
multinationals are behind the fighting, but we simply don't
see any evidence of that. In fact, the Pentagon seems to WANT
us to believe it, whether it is true or not.

The idea that the US is involved in Afghan fighting simply
because the military-industrial complex needs to be put to
work is perhaps a more sophisticated and credible argument.
But it still doesn't make a lot of sense. If NATO and the Pentagon wanted to fight endless wars, they could fight them anywhere. Why Afghanistan and Pakistan?

We would argue that the real reason to fight in Afghanistan has to do with control of the "navel of the world." The
war on terror is certainly manufactured but the powers that
be may have put it to good use, from their perspective, re-
gardless.

The Afghan Pashtuns and the Pakistan Punjabis are among a few tribes in the world that are not entirely subservient—at the top anyway—to Western interests.

Within this context, the failed Kabul Bank is an important element of control. The US and NATO are evidently and obviously trying hard to change the Afghan culture. Western finance, Western agriculture, Western education . . . all are being grafted onto the Afghan/Pashtun culture. If the war is merely for purposes of enriching the military-industrial complex, why bother?

The fall of Kabul Bank is symbolic of the shambles of this strategy, however. It reminds us of the larger dysfunctional nature of the war and the West's strategy. If we are correct, the powers that be badly want to win this war and the lack of success in changing the local culture is symptomatic of the struggle's larger futility.

That does not mean the war has not been fought for the sake of making war. Only that there are other reasons as well. Sometimes a war is what it seems to be—a methodology of conquest. And in this case, it's not one the West is winning.

> *"So dominant and problematic is the opium economy in Afghanistan today that a question Washington has avoided for the past nine years must be asked: Can anyone pacify a full-blown narco-state?"*

Afghanistan Needs to Transition from Opium to Other Crops

Alfred McCoy

Alfred McCoy is the J.R.W. Smail Professor of History at the University of Wisconsin-Madison. He is the author of The Politics of Heroin: CIA Complicity in the Global Drug Trade. *In the following viewpoint, he writes that Afghanistan has become reliant on opium production for half its economy, in part due to US policy for the last thirty years. This creates enormous incentives for corruption and provides funding for the Taliban insurgency. He concludes that the only way to end the conflict in Pakistan is to rebuild the devastated rural economy and irrigation systems so that the country can move from poppies to other crops.*

As you read, consider the following questions:

1. According to McCoy, when did opium first emerge as a key force in Afghan politics?

2. What does McCoy say was the Taliban's most important innovation in terms of opium production?

3. What is the cause of recent declines in opium production in Afghanistan, according to McCoy?

In ways that have escaped most observers, the [Barack] Obama administration is now trapped in an endless cycle of drugs and death in Afghanistan from which there is neither an easy end nor an obvious exit.

Heroin Capital of the World

After a year of cautious debate and costly deployments, President Obama finally launched his new Afghan war strategy at 2:40 A.M. on February 13, 2010, in a remote market town called Marjah in southern Afghanistan's Helmand province. As a wave of helicopters descended on Marjah's outskirts spitting up clouds of dust, hundreds of U.S. Marines dashed through fields sprouting opium poppies toward the town's mud-walled compounds.

After a week of fighting, U.S. war commander General Stanley A. McChrystal choppered into town with Afghanistan's vice president and Helmand's provincial governor. Their mission: a media rollout for the general's new-look counterinsurgency strategy based on bringing government to remote villages just like Marjah.

At a carefully staged meet and greet with some 200 villagers, however, the vice president and provincial governor faced some unexpected, unscripted anger. "If they come with tractors," one Afghani widow announced to a chorus of supportive shouts from her fellow farmers, "they will have to roll over me and kill me before they can kill my poppy."

For these poppy growers and thousands more like them, the return of government control, however contested, brought with it a perilous threat: opium eradication.

Throughout all the shooting and shouting, American commanders seemed strangely unaware that Marjah might qualify as the world's heroin capital—with hundreds of laboratories, reputedly hidden inside the area's mud-brick houses, regularly processing the local poppy crop into high-grade heroin. After all, the surrounding fields of Helmand province produce a remarkable 40% of the world's illicit opium supply, and much of this harvest has been traded in Marjah. Rushing through those opium fields to attack the [militant Islamic] Taliban on day one of this offensive, the Marines missed their real enemy, the ultimate force behind the Taliban insurgency, as they pursued just the latest crop of peasant guerrillas whose guns and wages are funded by those poppy plants. "You can't win this war," said one U.S. embassy official just back from inspecting these opium districts, "without taking on drug production in Helmand province."

Indeed, as Air Force One headed for Kabul Sunday, National Security Advisor James L. Jones assured reporters that President Obama would try to persuade Afghan president Hamid Karzai to prioritize "battling corruption, taking the fight to the narco-traffickers." The drug trade, he added, "provides a lot of the economic engine for the insurgents."

Just as these Marjah farmers spoiled General McChrystal's media event, so their crop has subverted every regime that has tried to rule Afghanistan for the past 30 years. During the CIA's [Central Intelligence Agency's] covert war in the 1980s, opium financed the *mujahedeen* or "freedom fighters" (as President Ronald Reagan called them) who finally forced the Soviets to abandon the country and then defeated its Marxist client state.

In the late 1990s, the Taliban, which had taken power in most of the country, lost any chance for international legitimacy by protecting and profiting from opium—and then, ironically, fell from power only months after reversing course and banning the crop. Since the US military intervened in 2001, a rising tide of opium has corrupted the government in Kabul while empowering a resurgent Taliban whose guerrillas have taken control of ever larger parts of the Afghan countryside.

Corrupted by Drugs

These three eras of almost constant warfare fueled a relentless rise in Afghanistan's opium harvest—from just 250 tons in 1979 to 8,200 tons in 2007. For the past five years, the Afghan opium harvest has accounted for as much as 50% of the country's gross domestic product (GDP) and provided the prime ingredient for over 90% of the world's heroin supply.

The ecological devastation and societal dislocation from these three war-torn decades has woven opium so deeply into the Afghan grain that it defies solution by Washington's best and brightest (as well as its most inept and least competent). Caroming between ignoring the opium crop and demanding its total eradication, the [George W.] Bush administration dithered for seven years while heroin boomed, and in doing so helped create a drug economy that corrupted and crippled the government of its ally, President Karzai. In recent years, opium farming has supported 500,000 Afghan families, nearly 20% of the country's estimated population, and funds a Taliban insurgency that has, since 2006, spread across the countryside.

To understand the Afghan war, one basic point must be grasped: In poor nations with weak state services, agriculture is the foundation for all politics, binding villagers to the government or warlords or rebels. The ultimate aim of counterinsurgency strategy is always to establish the state's authority. When the economy is illicit and by definition beyond government control, this task becomes monumental. If the insurgents capture that illicit economy, as the Taliban have done, then the task becomes little short of insurmountable.

Opium is an illegal drug, but Afghanistan's poppy crop is still grounded in networks of social trust that tie people together at each step in the chain of production. Crop loans are necessary for planting, labor exchange for harvesting, stability for marketing, and security for shipment. So dominant and problematic is the opium economy in Afghanistan today that a question Washington has avoided for the past nine years must be asked: Can anyone pacify a full-blown narco-state?

The answer to this critical question lies in the history of the three Afghan wars in which Washington has been involved over the past 30 years—the CIA covert warfare of the 1980s, the civil war of the 1990s (fueled at its start by $900 million in CIA funding), and since 2001, the U.S. invasion, occupation, and counterinsurgency campaigns. In each of these conflicts, Washington has tolerated drug trafficking by its Afghan allies as the price of military success—a policy of benign neglect that has helped make Afghanistan today the world's number one narco-state.

CIA Covert Warfare, Spreading Poppy Fields, and Drug Labs: The 1980s

Opium first emerged as a key force in Afghan politics during the CIA covert war against the Soviets, the last in a series of secret operations that it conducted along the mountain rimlands of Asia which stretch for 5,000 miles from Turkey to Thailand. In the late 1940s, as the Cold War was revving up, the United States first mounted covert probes of communism's Asian underbelly. For 40 years thereafter, the CIA fought a succession of secret wars along this mountain rim—in Burma [also known as Myanmar] during the 1950s, Laos in the 1960s, and Afghanistan in the 1980s. In one of history's ironic accidents, the southern reach of Communist China and the Soviet Union had coincided with Asia's opium zone along this

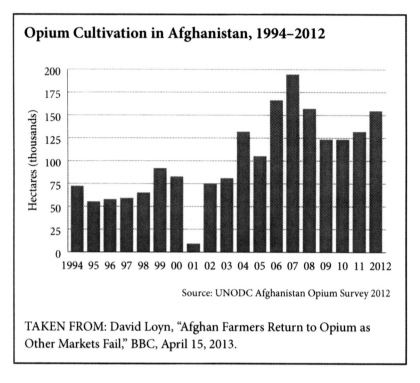

Opium Cultivation in Afghanistan, 1994–2012

Source: UNODC Afghanistan Opium Survey 2012

TAKEN FROM: David Loyn, "Afghan Farmers Return to Opium as Other Markets Fail," BBC, April 15, 2013.

same mountain rim, drawing the CIA into ambiguous alliances with the region's highland warlords.

Washington's first Afghan war began in 1979, when the Soviet Union invaded the country to save a Marxist client regime in Kabul, the Afghan capital. Seeing an opportunity to wound its Cold War enemy, the [Ronald] Reagan administration worked closely with Pakistan's military dictatorship in a ten-year CIA campaign to expel the Soviets.

This was, however, a covert operation unlike any other in the Cold War years. First, the collision of CIA secret operations and Soviet conventional warfare led to the devastation of Afghanistan's fragile highland ecology, damaging its traditional agriculture beyond immediate recovery, and fostering a growing dependence on the international drug trade. Of equal import, instead of conducting this covert warfare on its own as it had in Laos in the Vietnam War years, the CIA outsourced much of the operation to Pakistan's Inter-Services Intelligence (ISI), which soon became a powerful and ever more problematic ally.

When the ISI proposed its Afghan client, Gulbuddin Hekmatyar, as overall leader of the anti-Soviet resistance, Washington—with few alternatives—agreed. Over the next 10 years, the CIA supplied some $2 billion to Afghanistan's *mujahedeen* through the ISI, half to Hekmatyar, a violent fundamentalist infamous for throwing acid at unveiled women at Kabul University and, later, murdering rival resistance leaders. As the CIA operation was winding down in May 1990, the *Washington Post* published a front-page article charging that its key ally, Hekmatyar, was operating a chain of heroin laboratories inside Pakistan under the protection of the ISI.

Although this area had zero heroin production in the mid-1970s, the CIA's covert war served as the catalyst that transformed the Afghan-Pakistan borderlands into the world's largest heroin producing region. As *mujahedeen* guerrillas captured prime agricultural areas inside Afghanistan in the early 1980s, they began collecting a revolutionary poppy tax from their peasant supporters.

Once the Afghan guerrillas brought the opium across the border, they sold it to hundreds of Pakistani heroin labs operating under the ISI's protection. Between 1981 and 1990, Afghanistan's opium production grew tenfold—from 250 tons to 2,000 tons. After just two years of covert CIA support for the Afghan guerrillas, the U.S. attorney general announced in 1981 that Pakistan was already the source of 60% of the American heroin supply. Across Europe and Russia, Afghan-Pakistani heroin soon captured an even larger share of local markets, while inside Pakistan itself the number of addicts soared from zero in 1979 to 1.2 million just five years later.

After investing $3 billion in Afghanistan's destruction, Washington just walked away in 1992, leaving behind a thoroughly ravaged country with over one million dead, five million refugees, 10–20 million land mines still in place, an infrastructure in ruins, an economy in tatters, and well-armed tribal warlords prepared to fight among themselves for control of the capital. Even when Washington finally cut its covert CIA funding at the end of 1991, however, Pakistan's ISI continued to back favored local warlords in pursuit of its long-term goal of installing a Pashtun client regime in Kabul.

Drug Lords, Dragon's Teeth, and Civil Wars: The 1990s

Throughout the 1990s, ruthless local warlords mixed guns and opium in a lethal brew as part of a brutal struggle for power. It was almost as if the soil had been sown with those dragons' teeth of ancient myth that can suddenly sprout into an army of full-grown warriors, who leap from the earth with swords drawn for war.

When northern resistance forces finally captured Kabul from the Communist regime, which had outlasted the Soviet withdrawal by three years, Pakistan still backed its client Hekmatyar. He, in turn, unleashed his artillery on the besieged capital. The result: The deaths of an estimated 50,000 more Afghans. Even a slaughter of such monumental proportions, however, could not win power for this unpopular fundamentalist. So the ISI armed a new force, the Taliban and in September 1996, it succeeded in capturing Kabul, only to fight the Northern Alliance for the next five years in the valleys to the north of the capital.

During this seemingly unending civil war, rival factions leaned heavily on opium to finance the fighting, more than doubling the harvest to 4,600 tons by 1999. Throughout these two decades of warfare and a twentyfold jump in drug production, Afghanistan itself was slowly transformed from a diverse agricultural ecosystem—with herding, orchards, and over 60 food crops—into the world's first economy dependent on the production of a single illicit drug. In the process, a fragile human ecology was brought to ruin in an unprecedented way. . . .

Without any aid to restock their herds, reseed their fields, or replant their orchards, Afghan farmers—including some 3 million returning refugees—found sustenance in opium, which had historically been but a small part of their agriculture.

Since poppy cultivation requires nine times more labor per hectare than wheat, opium offered immediate seasonal employment to more than a million Afghans—perhaps half of those actually employed at the time. In this ruined land and ravaged economy, opium merchants alone could accumulate capital rapidly and so give poppy farmers crop loans equivalent to more than half their annual incomes, credit critical to the survival of many poor villagers.

In marked contrast to the marginal yields the country's harsh climate offers most food crops, Afghanistan proved ideal for opium. On average, each hectare of Afghan poppy land produces three to five times more than its chief competitor, Burma. Most important of all, in such an arid ecosystem, subject to periodic drought, opium uses less than half the water needed for staples such as wheat.

After taking power in 1996, the Taliban regime encouraged a nationwide expansion of opium cultivation, doubling production to 4,600 tons, then equivalent to 75% of the world's heroin supply. Signaling its support for drug production, the Taliban regime began collecting a 20% tax from the yearly opium harvest, earning an estimated $100 million in revenues.

In retrospect, the regime's most important innovation was undoubtedly the introduction of large-scale heroin refining in the environs of the city of Jalalabad. There, hundreds of crude labs set to work, paying only a modest production tax of $70 on every kilo of heroin powder. According to U.N. [United Nations] researchers, the Taliban also presided over bustling regional opium markets in Helmand and Nangarhar provinces, protecting some 240 top traders there.

During the 1990s, Afghanistan's soaring opium harvest fueled an international smuggling trade that tied central Asia, Russia, and Europe into a vast illicit market of arms, drugs, and money laundering. It also helped fuel an eruption of ethnic insurgency across a 3,000-mile swath of land from Uzbekistan in central Asia to Bosnia in the Balkans.

In July 2000, however, the Taliban leader Mullah [Mohammed] Omar suddenly ordered a ban on all opium cultivation in a desperate bid for international recognition. Remarkably enough, almost overnight the Taliban regime used the ruthless repression for which it was infamous to slash the opium harvest by 94% to only 185 metric tons.

By then, however, Afghanistan had become dependent on poppy production for most of its taxes, export income, and employment. In effect, the Taliban's ban was an act of economic suicide that brought an already weakened society to the brink of collapse. This was the unwitting weapon the U.S. wielded when it began its military campaign against the Taliban in October 2001. Without opium, the regime was already a hollow shell and essentially imploded at the bursting of the first American bombs.

The Return of the CIA, Opium, and Counterinsurgency: 2001

To defeat the Taliban in the aftermath of 9/11 [referring to the terrorist attacks on the United States on September 11, 2001], the CIA successfully mobilized former warlords long active in the heroin trade to seize towns and cities across eastern Afghanistan. In other words, the agency and its local allies created ideal conditions for reversing the Taliban's opium ban and reviving the drug traffic. Only weeks after the collapse of the Taliban, officials were reporting an outburst of poppy planting in the heroin heartlands of Helmand and Nangarhar.

At a Tokyo international donors' conference in January 2002, Hamid Karzai, the new prime minister put in place by the Bush administration, issued a *pro forma* ban on opium growing—without any means of enforcing it against the power of these resurgent local warlords. . . .

After five years of the U.S. occupation, Afghanistan's drug production had swelled to unprecedented proportions. In August 2007, the U.N. reported that the country's record opium crop covered almost 500,000 acres, an area larger than all the coca fields in Latin America. From a modest 185 tons at the start of American intervention in 2001, Afghanistan now produced 8,200 tons of opium, a remarkable 53% of the country's GDP and 93% of global heroin supply.

In this way, Afghanistan became the world's first true "narco-state." If a cocaine traffic that provided just 3% of Colombia's GDP could bring in its wake endless violence and powerful cartels capable of corrupting that country's government, then we can only imagine the consequences of Afghanistan's dependence on opium for more than 50% of its entire economy.

At a drug conference in Kabul this month [in March 2010], the head of Russia's federal narcotics service estimated the value of Afghanistan's current opium crop at $65 billion. Only $500 million of that vast sum goes to Afghanistan's farmers, $300 million to the Taliban guerrillas, and the $64 billion balance "to the drug mafia," leaving ample funds to corrupt the Karzai government in a nation whose total GDP is only $10 billion.

Indeed, opium's influence is so pervasive that many Afghan officials, from village leaders to Kabul's police chief, the defense minister, and the president's brother, have been tainted by the traffic. So cancerous and crippling is this corruption that, according to recent U.N. estimates, Afghans are forced to spend a stunning $2.5 billion in bribes. Not surprisingly, the government's repeated attempts at opium eradication have been thoroughly compromised by what the U.N. has called "corrupt deals between field owners, village elders, and eradication teams."

Not only have drug taxes funded an expanding guerrilla force, but the Taliban's role in protecting opium farmers and the heroin merchants who rely on their crop gives them real control over the core of the country's economy. In January 2009, the U.N. and anonymous U.S. "intelligence officials" estimated that drug traffic provided Taliban insurgents with $400 million a year. "Clearly," commented Defense Secretary Robert M. Gates, "we have to go after the drug labs and the drug lords that provide support to the Taliban and other insurgents."

In mid-2009, the U.S. embassy launched a multiagency effort, called the Afghan Threat Finance Cell, to cut Taliban drug monies through financial controls. But one American official soon compared this effort to "punching Jell-O." By August 2009, a frustrated Obama administration had ordered the U.S. military to "kill or capture" 50 Taliban-connected drug lords who were placed on a classified "kill list."

Since the record crop of 2007, opium production has, in fact, declined somewhat—to 6,900 tons last year (still over 90% of the world's opium supply). While U.N. analysts attribute this 20% reduction largely to eradication efforts, a more likely cause has been the global glut of heroin that came with the Afghan opium boom, and which had depressed the price of poppies by 34%. In fact, even this reduced Afghan opium crop is still far above total world demand, which the U.N. estimates at 5,000 tons per annum.

Preliminary reports on the 2010 Afghan opium harvest, which starts next month, indicate that the drug problem is not going away. Some U.S. officials who have surveyed Helmand's opium heartland see signs of an expanded crop. Even the U.N. drug experts who have predicted a continuing decline in production are not optimistic about long-term trends. Opium prices might decline for a few years, but the price of wheat and other staple crops is dropping even faster, leaving poppies as by far the most profitable crop for poor Afghan farmers.

Ending the Cycle of Drugs and Death

With its forces now planted in the dragon's teeth soil of Afghanistan, Washington is locked into what looks to be an unending cycle of drugs and death. Every spring in those rugged mountains, the snows melt, the opium seeds sprout, and a fresh crop of Taliban fighters takes to the field, many to die by lethal American fire. And the next year, the snows melt again, fresh poppy shoots break through the soil, and a new crop of teenaged Taliban fighters pick up arms against America, spilling more blood. This cycle has been repeated for the past ten years and, unless something changes, can continue indefinitely.

Is there any alternative? Even were the cost of rebuilding Afghanistan's rural economy—with its orchards, flocks, and food crops—as high as $30 billion or, for that matter, $90 billion dollars, the money is at hand. By conservative estimates, the cost of President Obama's ongoing surge of 30,000 troops alone is $30 billion a year. So just bringing those 30,000 troops home would create ample funds to begin the rebuilding of rural life in Afghanistan, making it possible for young farmers to begin feeding their families without joining the Taliban's army.

Short of another precipitous withdrawal akin to 1991, Washington has no realistic alternative to the costly, long-term reconstruction of Afghanistan's agriculture. Beneath the gaze of an allied force that now numbers about 120,000 soldiers, opium has fueled the Taliban's growth into an omnipresent shadow government and an effective guerrilla army. The idea that our expanded military presence might soon succeed in driving back that force and handing over pacification to the illiterate, drug-addicted Afghan police and army remains, for the time being, a fantasy. Quick fixes like paying poppy farmers not to plant, something British and Americans have both tried, can backfire and end up actually promoting yet more opium cultivation. Rapid drug eradication without alternative employment, something the private contractor DynCorp [International] tried so disastrously under a $150 million contract in 2005, would simply plunge Afghanistan into more misery, stoking mass anger and destabilizing the Kabul government further.

So the choice is clear enough: We can continue to fertilize this deadly soil with yet more blood in a brutal war with an uncertain outcome—for both the United States and the people of Afghanistan. Or we can begin to withdraw American forces while helping renew this ancient, arid land by replanting its orchards, replenishing its flocks, and rebuilding the irrigation systems ruined in decades of war.

At this point, our only realistic choice is this sort of serious rural development—that is, reconstructing the Afghan countryside through countless small-scale projects until food crops become a viable alternative to opium. To put it simply, so simply that even Washington might understand, you can only pacify a narco-state when it is no longer a narco-state.

> "Producing licit opioids for export would link Afghanistan to the global trading system and provide a legal and lucrative pathway toward economic development."

Poppies for Pain Relief

Charli Carpenter

Charli Carpenter is an associate professor in the Department of Political Science at the University of Massachusetts Amherst. In the following viewpoint, she argues that there is a serious shortage of analgesics, or painkillers, worldwide and that this shortage is especially acute in the developing world. Rather than working to eradicate Afghanistan's poppy crop to prevent it from being used for illegal heroin, Carpenter says, Afghan poppies could be channeled into legal pain reduction. This would help many worldwide who need painkillers and could also help stabilize Afghanistan's economy.

As you read, consider the following questions:

1. What is the result of the analgesic shortage in India?

2. What policy does Carpenter say fuels the shortage of analgesics?

Charli Carpenter, "Poppies for Pain Relief," *Lawyers, Guns, and Money*, April 7, 2011.

3. According to Carpenter, what factors other than low supply contribute to the analgesic shortage?

Millions of individuals worldwide suffer from acute or chronic pain without adequate access to pain medication. The problem is particularly acute in the developing world, as *Time* magazine chronicled last year:

> Whether you will have access to pain treatment depends largely upon where you live. Africa, which has most of the world's AIDS victims, is a painkiller wasteland. In India, more than a million cancer and AIDS sufferers die each year in extreme pain as cumbersome regulations and paperwork make it nearly impossible to get prescription painkillers. (India produces much of the world's legal opium, yet nearly all of it is exported to Western pharmaceutical companies.)

> The geography of pain relief is so skewed that the seven richest countries consume 84% of the world's supply of legal opiates, according to the International Narcotics Control Board, an independent agency that enforces U.N. conventions. For the estimated 10 million people who are suffering from untreated pain, relief is often found only on the black market, or in death.

This gaping unmet need and global inequity is becoming the subject of various calls for change, by pain experts, by cancer treatment advocates, by international organizations, and by the human rights community. As Brent Foster explains in this podcast,* the reasons behind the inequitable global distribution of pain medication are complex—like many intractable global social problems that get too little attention by policy makers.

However, a significant (and solvable) aspect of the problem is simply the relationship of supply to demand: The need for analgesics like morphine far outweighs the available supply. In part, this is due to the fact that such analgesics are produced from opium, the sap of the poppy. Since the same plant

The Discovery of Opium

Opium has been used by man since prehistoric times and was arguably the first drug to be discovered. Being naturally occurring, it almost certainly predates the discovery of alcohol which requires a knowledge of fermentation.

The preserved remains of cultivated poppy seeds and pods have been discovered in the sites of fourth millennium B.C. Neolithic pile-dwelling villages in Switzerland. Botanical examination has shown these not to be *Papaver setigerum*, but *Papaver somniferum* or possibly a deliberate hybrid. As these ancient farmers also grew linseed, it is likely both crops were utilised for their oil although no suitable contemporary tools for oil extraction have been found and it is, therefore, just as likely the poppy was grown for its narcotic effect, either as a painkiller or for use in religious ceremonies—or for both.

It has long been suggested that the knowledge of opium spread from Egypt through Asia Minor to the rest of the Old World but the Swiss discoveries cast this theory into doubt. What is as likely is that the secret of opium originated in the eastern reaches of Europe—in the Balkans or around the Black Sea—and spread south and west from there.

Martin Booth, Opium: A History.
New York: St. Martin's Press, 1996.

extract can also be used to produce heroin, a significant amount of political effort is now being expended worldwide to actually inhibit, rather than encourage, opioid production. This fuels shortages of analgesics.

Writing in the *Journal of Epidemiology and Community Health*, Amir Attaran and Andrew Boozary suggest a seldom-mentioned way to increase supply: reframing Afghanistan's poppy problem as "an opportunity for global public health." In short, the authors suggest pro-government forces abandon efforts to eradicate Afghan poppy cultivation and instead redirect them toward the production of licit opioids for analgesic pain medication.

> Opium can be extracted to produce morphine at a conservative ratio of 10:1, and morphine in turn can be synthesised into other medical analgesics (e.g., codeine or dihydromorphine) with little loss. As such, Afghanistan's available poppy crop is sufficient to supply about 690 tons of morphine: enough to nearly triple the current global supply of that medicine, and to narrow substantially the analgesia gap between rich- and poor-country patients having terminal cancer or HIV/AIDS pain.

> No other country comes remotely close to producing enough. As such, the 'problem' of Afghanistan's opium poppy, which is now wasted on manufacturing illicit drugs, is potentially the solution for millions of suffering pain patients, who desperately need proper analgesic medicines.

Of course, increasing supply would ultimately be only one important step in resolving the global distribution problem, which is partly a result of a grossly inequitable quota system operated by the UN International Narcotics Control Board, as well as cultural factors.

But given the staggering human need for opioid analgesics worldwide, it is remarkable that policy discourse on Afghan poppy production has been so focused on eradication, reduction or poppy-free zones to the exclusion of regulation for the purpose of filling medical need. *Foreign Policy*'s recent "Think Again" piece on Afghanistan's poppy crop, for example, ignores this option completely, suggesting only marginal shifts in status quo policies that treat poppies as the problem (like "focusing alternative-development efforts on more stable parts of the country" or "fund drug treatment in Afghanistan.")

Producing licit opioids for export would link Afghanistan to the global trading system and provide a legal and lucrative pathway toward economic development. Instead, poppy crops are being literally destroyed in Afghanistan as part of the "war on drugs."

Editor Note:

* "The Global Fight for Pain Relief," a podcast for Human Rights Watch

> "We are already taking measures to ensure that the blow to the Afghan economy from the reduction in international forces and international assistance are taken into account."

Afghanistan Is Making Substantial Economic Progress

J. Alexander Thier as told to Jayshree Bajoria

J. Alexander Thier is assistant to the administrator for policy, planning, and learning at the United States Agency for International Development (USAID). He formerly served as assistant to the administrator for Afghanistan and Pakistan affairs at US-AID. Jayshree Bajoria is the South Asia researcher at Human Rights Watch and former deputy editor at CFR.org. In the following viewpoint, Thier says that the Afghan economy has made enormous strides since the US invasion in 2001. He says that USAID continues to work to make sure funds go to rebuilding rather than to corruption. He concludes that the US withdrawal will be a difficult moment for Afghanistan's economy, but he says that increased aid and careful use of funds should allow Afghanistan to continue to develop.

As you read, consider the following questions:

1. What specific achievements does Thier point to in the realms of education and health in Afghanistan?

2. Why is it so difficult to get Afghan crops to market, according to Thier?

3. What strides does Thier say Afghanistan has made in the ten years since he lived in the country in the 1990s?

Serious concerns persist in the international community about Afghanistan's governance abilities as the 2014 time line for the security transition to Afghan forces draws near. The director of the office of Afghanistan and Pakistan affairs at the [United States] Agency for International Development [USAID], J. Alexander Thier, says economic effects of the drawdown "will be real" but points to sweeping improvements in Afghanistan's capacity to govern itself, singling out progress in health, education, energy, and road building. "We are changing the way we do business by doing more of our work directly through the Afghan government," to increase spending that goes directly into the Afghan economy, he says. Going forward, he says, investment in infrastructure and energy will be critical to increasing Afghans' capacity and making economic growth sustainable. He says the international community will be supporting development work in Afghanistan for years beyond 2014.

What's Working in Afghanistan?

Jayshree Bajoria: What's working from the standpoint of USAID in Afghanistan, and what are the problem areas?

J. Alexander Thier: We've had significant development achievements in the last ten years in the area of health and education. We've gone from having less than 10 percent of Afghans having access to any type of basic health services to nearly 80 percent. The same is true in the sphere of education, where under the Taliban less than one million children—almost all boys—were in school. Today, you have over eight million children in school, 35 percent of whom are girls.

Going forward, we are looking at a few key areas for investment in Afghanistan, what we call our "foundational investments." They're foundational because we know we have resources today that we might not have in five years, so we want to make sure that we're giving Afghans capacity economically, from an infrastructure point of view, to really carry their own future forward and become increasingly self-sufficient.

We've made enormous investments in roads, building something like 1,800 kilometers of roads, and we are making an investment in energy. One of the most important areas in economic growth is agriculture. One of the huge problems that agriculture faces in Afghanistan is in terms of access to water, but particularly in terms of getting the crops to market. There is a nearly 50 percent spoilage rate for goods that are grown in Afghanistan because the roads are bad, and people don't have cold storage, access to market, [or] access to properly dry and store foodstuffs for export. So, our ability to improve that value chain for food in Afghanistan is critical for food security, it's critical for economic growth, and it will depend upon improved infrastructure in the country.

In the longer term, Afghanistan is going to rely on mineral resources in part to increase its revenues, and it will also rely on trade from other countries. We're working hard on improving trade, particularly with Pakistan at the moment but also throughout the region. We're also working on making sure that Afghanistan has an environment that is conducive to investment, that is conducive to extraction in a way that will have positive benefits for the economy and avoid some of the other problems that many third world countries have had when they get sudden access to wealth that can undermine governance.

How are you doing that? And how do you ensure that the aid dollars don't feed into the insurgency?

[P]eople should not be viewing the U.S. commitment to Afghanistan as one that's limited by 2014.

When I joined USAID in the summer of 2010, I got a report about a project where funds may have been siphoned off for illicit power structures or insurgents. I asked the staff how we could ensure that that wasn't happening and what we can do in the future. As a result, we launched the Accountable Assistance for Afghanistan (A3) initiative, and this is essentially adding several layers of accountability to the process of contracting and development work that we have in Afghanistan.

We put in place a vetting process that has access to a large number of databases and classified information, so that we can look at the Afghan partners that we're employing to make sure they don't fall into the category of organizations or people who we don't want funding going to.

One of the problems that we have contractually in Afghanistan, and around the world, is that when you have multiple subcontracts, we lose sight of where the money is going, who it's going to, or whether it's being cost-effective. One of the ways in which we can maintain a much tighter focus and accountability is to limit the number of subcontracts.

We're enhancing our capacity not only to measure outputs from our project but also looking at outcomes. One of the ways is looking at the question of sustainability. We don't want to spend money on projects that are not going to be sustainable. [We want to ensure that] there will be money in place to support those programs in the long term from the Afghan budget, [and] that the Afghans themselves own the project and can maintain it. One of the critical things that we've done in the last two years is to build DABS [Da Afghanistan Breshna Sherkat], the electric utility. That didn't really exist before, [and] today has the capacity to maintain

Progress in Female Education

Female education has faced significant obstacles in Afghanistan, yet there have been enormous gains since 2001. Under the Taliban, the majority of girls' schools were closed and gross enrollment fell from 32% to just 6.4%. In the early years after the fall of the Taliban, education was a top priority for the Afghan government and donors. Much of this donor focus was on getting children back into school, with a particular emphasis on primary level. The Back to School campaign, launched in 2002, significantly expanded enrollment, which has increased nearly sevenfold, from approximately 900,000 in 2000 to 6.7 million in 2009. For girls, the increase has been even more dramatic; official enrollment figures have increased from an estimated 5,000 under the Taliban to 2.4 million girls currently enrolled.

Many of the girls enrolled through the Back to School campaign are now completing primary school. Yet beginning in 2006, efforts to improve education in Afghanistan began to slow down. Nearly five years on, those efforts have nearly run out of steam. A new approach from both the Afghan government and donors is urgently required to hold onto the gains that have been made.

Ashley Jackson,
"High Stakes: Girls' Education in Afghanistan,"
Joint NGO Briefing Paper, February 24, 2011, p. 4.

their existing investments, and has doubled its revenue generation every year for the last three years.

The 2014 Transition

As we look to the transition in 2014, do you think the Afghans have the capacity to take over?

One of the things that people don't appreciate is how dramatically far Afghanistan has come in the last ten years, in terms of the capacity for governance. In the 1990s, when I lived there for four years during the civil war, it was like Somalia. It was warring fiefdoms; there really wasn't a government. But now, ten years on into the intervention, there are some very heartening signs of the ability of Afghans to handle their country. I went, for instance, recently to the Afghan civil service academy, and what you see are hundreds of young Afghans learning a variety of basic management skills. It's not sexy: it's accounting, it's budgeting, and it's the basic level of competence that you need in civil servants to serve in Kabul and around the country. That cadre of people did not exist ten years ago.

[T]here are already steps we are taking to mitigate the economic effects of the drawdown, but those effects will be real.

Another example is the cell phone network and industry. You could count the number of phones in Afghanistan on your hands a decade ago. Today, some 85 percent of Afghans have access to the cellular networks; some 60 percent are on and using the networks. We have a program that sends information to farmers about price and weather. We have just launched in Kabul an initiative to increase the amount of payments that people can make through their cell phones. Only 3 percent of Afghans have access [to financial services] or have a bank account; whereas 85 percent have access to the cell network. So, enabling them to make payments through the cell phone is actually going to blow wide open financial inclusion in Afghanistan.

Given the levels of corruption in the [President Hamid] Karzai government and the rifts with the United States, do you still think that by 2014 the country will have put in place political and economic institutions needed for transition?

In many respects, Afghans have already taken over some of these responsibilities, and some of them will continue to be dependent upon the international community for years to come. Even as Afghanistan makes it through this process, it will still be one of the poorest countries in the world, having come out of decades of conflict. So, people should not be viewing the U.S. commitment to Afghanistan as one that's limited by 2014.

Preventing Depression

There are a number of projects aimed at economic growth, but what is the time line for such projects? Especially given the warning sounded by a June Senate Foreign Relations Committee report that the Afghan economy could slide into a depression with the decline of foreign development spending?

We are already taking measures to ensure that the blow to the Afghan economy from the reduction in international forces and international assistance are taken into account.

Let me give you an example. When we spend money for development programs through local entities or through the Afghan budget, a lot of that money makes it into the local economy. When we spend that money through external entities, contractors and so on, less of it makes it into the local economy. So, when we look at USAID resources and probably much more importantly military resources, if we can increase the amount of spending that goes into the economy even as our overall input decreases, we can maintain for a number of years a relatively steady input of funds that are hitting the Afghan economy. So, we are changing the way we do business by doing more of our work directly through the Afghan government.

We committed in July 2010 at the Kabul conference to try to meet the goal of 50 percent of our funds in Afghanistan to go through the Afghan budget. That doesn't mean that we give the Afghans the money, but what it does mean is that we work with Afghan ministries, and that money gets programmed through specific institutions. So, there are already steps we are taking to mitigate the economic effects of the drawdown, but those effects will be real. We have to continue looking for opportunities through economic growth, in other words increase the amount that Afghans themselves are earning, and other such initiatives like more local spending in the economy to lessen [the negative effects of the drawdown].

> *"People are waiting because they don't know what will happen after the elections. . . . They're keeping the money. Even if some projects are completed 50 percent, they've stopped work."*

Afghanistan's Economy Continues to Struggle as a Result of War

Gopal Ratnam

Gopal Ratnam is a reporter for Bloomberg News. In the following viewpoint, he reports on the problems that Afghanistan's economy faces as coalition forces plan to pull out of the country. He says that uncertainty about the future has slowed investment. Ongoing insecurity, fear of a Taliban victory, and the failure to stem the opium trade are other serious challenges. However, he says, some Afghans remain positive, looking to trade and future mineral exploitation as a way to turn the country's economy around.

As you read, consider the following questions:

1. What are the World Bank's projections for Afghan growth in 2014?

2. What is needed to explore and extract Afghanistan's mineral riches, according to Ratnam?

3. Who is Ismail Ghazanfar, and in what economic projects is he involved in Afghanistan?

Afghanistan's economy remains hostage to the country's politics and security after more than a dozen years of American intervention.

Mahmood Hanifi sees it every day in his tile shop in Kandahar city. Sales, he said, have fallen by half in two years because customers are postponing home remodeling projects until after Afghanistan's April 5 [2014] presidential election and the departure of most international troops by the end of next year.

"People are waiting because they don't know what will happen after the elections," Hanifi said through an interpreter, looking out from a glass-enclosed cubicle onto his showroom of marble and ceramic tiles decorated with designs and Islamic inscriptions. "They're keeping the money. Even if some projects are completed 50 percent, they've stopped work."

The World Bank predicts that Afghanistan's economic growth will decline to 3.1 percent this year [2014] from 14 percent last year as consumers, entrepreneurs and investors can only guess what's ahead for a nation long dependent on foreign troops and aid, with mineral resources that have never been tapped and agriculture still dominated by opium exports.

"The upside in Afghanistan is very unclear, but the downside is very clear," said Ahmad Bassam, managing director of Kabul-based Afghan Holding Group, an investment advisory firm. "If the [Islamic militant] Taliban take over, we'll all leave," he said of Afghan investors, many of whom already have second homes in Dubai [Saudi Arabia] and regularly move much of their money there.

The outflow of capital from Afghanistan since 2009, including the proceeds of illegal drug trafficking, has roughly equaled American financial assistance in the same period, according to two U.S. officials who asked not to be identified discussing a classified estimate.

Karzai Balking

Afghan president Hamid Karzai's refusal so far to sign a security agreement that would permit some U.S. and coalition forces to remain in his country beyond 2014 is exacerbating the economic anxiety.

For the fiscal year that ended in March, 78 percent of Afghanistan's development budget and 44 percent of its security budget came from international aid and donor agencies, according to the ministry of finance. Failure to reach a security agreement would jeopardize pledges of as much as $10 billion a year in economic and military assistance through 2017.

Without a security agreement in place, "we've seen capital flight," Marine Corps General Joseph Dunford, the top commander of U.S. and allied forces in Afghanistan, told reporters in Kabul this month. "We've seen real estate prices go down."

Registrations of new companies declined 43 percent in the first seven months of this year, to 2,000 from 3,500 in the same period a year earlier, according to the World Bank, citing data from Afghanistan Investment Support Agency.

For Afghan entrepreneurs such as Mustafa Sadiq, business decisions are a daily exercise in country risk assessment. They must weigh the approaching departure of U.S. and allied combat forces after 12 years, the threat of attacks by resurgent terrorist groups, persistent corruption and uncertainty over who will succeed Karzai, who's ruled for 10 years.

In 2009, Sadiq said, he invested $25 million from his family's century-old imports business to start Omaid Bahar Fruits Processing Ltd., which makes concentrates and juices from pomegranates, apples and other fruits in an industrial park in Kabul. This year, Sadiq said sales have dropped as much as 40 percent.

"Business is declining rapidly because of uncertainty after 2014, as Afghan buyers do not earn as they used to, and that's why they spend less," he said in a phone interview.

Under Capacity

The plant, which employs 450 workers, was damaged in a December 2012 suicide car-bomb attack, forcing him to spend $7 million to rebuild, Sadiq said. While the project was completed two months ago, the factory still runs at only 40 percent of capacity, he said.

Sadiq said he's put on hold a planned $70 million expansion to produce yogurt and fruit-flavored milk products because of the attack, falling demand and a lack of official support. He said the government canceled plans to give him a three-year tax break for the plant's losses in the bombing.

Afghanistan's unemployment rate reached an estimated 40 percent in 2012, Abdul Hadi Arghandiwal, the country's economy minister, said in a phone interview. He said the jobless rate may climb to 50 percent with the loss of work for Afghans as international forces and their contractors depart.

Creating jobs through private investment will be a "mammoth, mammoth task" for the Afghan government, said Ken Yamashita, the Kabul-based coordinating director for the U.S. Agency for International Development, which has spent about $17 billion on development programs in Afghanistan since 2002.

"If you think about the employment that needs to be generated, it's about 150,000 to 200,000 jobs needed per year," Yamashita said in a phone interview.

Big enterprises—including exploring and extracting Afghanistan's mineral riches, valued by the Pentagon and the U.S. Geological Survey at about $1 trillion—will require a substantial investment in infrastructure that will take years to build, according to Vahid Alaghband, founder and chairman of London-based Balli Group Plc, which has about four decades of experience in mining projects in central and eastern Europe and South America.

Alaghband was among a group of international investors who visited Afghanistan in June on a trip arranged by McKinsey & Co., the New York–based consulting firm, and the Pentagon's Task Force for Business and Stability Operations.

Starting Small

After examining the prospects for mining, Alaghband said he decided to start small with an investment in the "millions, not hundreds of millions" of dollars to create a network of print and publishing shops in Afghanistan, as well as a chain of auto dealerships.

Beginning in 2014, executives from the Balli Group's operations in Dubai will "roll out the two sets of businesses into Afghanistan to see how it goes and learn about the place," Alaghband said.

In meetings with investors, Afghan officials talked about "export of agricultural products and other agricommodities," Alaghband said. "Those things may generate about $1 billion of exports each year, but won't fill the massive gap that military spending will leave" when international troops depart the country.

Opium remains Afghanistan's most lucrative agricultural export, and U.S. officials have acknowledged that the effort to eradicate it has failed. Opium production "remains a substantial portion of overall agricultural output and will continue to fuel corruption and fund the insurgency," the Pentagon said in a report to Congress last month.

In addition to fighting insurgents, U.S. and coalition forces ran development projects and health care clinics, provided grants and brought in agricultural experts, said Barna Karimi,

Mining Won't Save Afghanistan

Typical physical start-up costs for major mine works in Afghanistan were estimated to run to $5 billion apiece. To take another not entirely facetious parallel, even the North Sea contains an estimated $207 billion of gold, but once start-up and extraction costs are taken into the equation, they render it a clearly uneconomical mining prospect. The degree of benefit in mineral extraction is also usually shorter term than in the oil or natural gas industries. Large-scale mine workings typically encounter the law of diminishing returns within a matter of a decade. Above all, the Western commitment to a sizeable security presence lasted only up to 2015 at the very latest, whereas the infrastructure and development time line for Afghanistan's mineral wealth required between ten and fifteen years of investment—up to 2025.

The mineral wealth story was a typical example of the hazy quick fixes and loose linkages that had characterized Western interest and activity in Afghanistan since 2001. Far from representing a genuine breakthrough, it marked merely the latest in a long line of supposed 'turning points' in the Western narrative regarding the country. . . .

Tim Bird and Alex Marshall, Afghanistan: How the West Lost Its Way. *New Haven, CT: Yale University Press, 2011.*

a former Afghan ambassador to Canada who's now managing director of Capitalize LLC, a Washington-based consulting and investment advisory firm.

"What is the substitute for all that?" Karimi said in an interview. "For Afghanistan, it's not clear who will fill the gap.

Although the government of Afghanistan should fill the gap, does it have the resources, the ability and capacity?"

Hanifi, the tile merchant, said the lack of reliable power hobbles business in his shop near Highway 1, which connects Kandahar to Kabul about 313 miles (504 kilometers) to the north.

He said he lacks a dependable source of power for machinery to cut the tiles he imports from Iran, Pakistan and China for his customers' kitchens and stairs. "If we don't have enough petrol or diesel, then we won't be able to have electricity from generators," he said.

Power Failure

A power failure in the wealthy Wazir Akbar Khan neighborhood of Kabul left the home of Afghan finance minister Omar Zakhilwal without electricity when he received a visiting reporter on a weekday morning. That didn't daunt Zakhilwal as he dismissed the grim prognosis others see for Afghanistan.

Exports of fresh and dried fruits, trade and transit, and service industries will help keep the economy going until the mineral and mining industries take off in the next decade, Zakhilwal said over a breakfast of eggs, fried potatoes, pomegranates and Afghan bread.

"Unfortunately, there's a doomsday analysis for Afghanistan which is not based on facts or reality on the ground," Zakhilwal said. "They compare Afghanistan of today with Afghanistan of 1992—the post-Soviet period. The international forces here are not the same as Soviet forces, and the people of Afghanistan are not the same people."

Zakhilwal's optimism is shared by Ismail Ghazanfar, chief executive officer of the Ghazanfar Group. He said his family business that began selling televisions in Afghanistan 40 years ago now employs more than 3,000 people at its refinery in Hairatan, near the border with Uzbekistan. The group also owns banks, mining and construction companies.

A group including Ghazanfar, the state-owned Turkish Petroleum Corp. and Dubai-based Dragon Oil Plc (DGO) won a $150 million bid in October to explore for gas in the Afghan-Tajikistan basin.

"It's completely risk capital," Ghazanfar said in an interview, referring to his company's 20 percent stake in the project. "If we discover gas, then we have to invest $1 billion."

The personal safety of investors is at greater risk than their investments are, said Ghazanfar, whose family lives most of the time in Dubai.

Security measures such as armed guards to protect against kidnappings and attacks add to the cost of doing business, Ghazanfar said, "but it's not so much that you can't accept it."

Periodical and Internet Sources Bibliography

The following articles have been selected to supplement the diverse views presented in this chapter.

Jeff Black	"Afghan Opium Production on the Rise Despite U.S. Troops, Inspector Says," NBC News, January 15, 2014.
Sean Carberry and Sultan Faizy	"Afghan Farmers: Opium Is the Only Way to Make a Living," NPR, November 14, 2013.
Graciana del Castillo	"Afghanistan's Misguided Economy," *Boston Review*, January 28, 2014.
Patrick Cockburn	"After 12 Years, £390bn, and Countless Dead, We Leave Poverty, Fraud—and the Taliban in Afghanistan," *Independent* (London), January 12, 2014.
Richard Ghiasy and Fraidoon Sekander	"Can Afghanistan's Economy Stand on Its Own?," *Diplomat*, January 30, 2014.
Emma Graham-Harrison	"UK Aid Projects in Afghanistan 'Must Improve in Order to Stem Poverty,'" *Guardian*, March 6, 2014.
Missy Ryan	"U.S. Aid Plan Seeks to Shield Afghanistan from End to War Economy," Reuters, February 9, 2014.
Kevin Sieff	"As U.S. War Ends, Russia Returns to Afghanistan with Series of Investment Projects," *Washington Post*, March 21, 2014.
Matt Sledge	"Watchdog Warns of Corruption as $1 Billion in U.S. Aid Flows to Afghanistan," *Huffington Post*, January 30, 2014.

OPPOSING
VIEWPOINTS®
SERIES

CHAPTER 4

What Is the Human Rights Situation in Afghanistan?

Chapter Preface

Women face many restrictions on their freedoms in Afghanistan and are often the targets of human rights abuses. Many inside and outside the country fear that the situation for women may worsen as Western forces withdraw from the country. These fears gained some support early in 2014 with the introduction into the Afghan legislature of a bill that would effectively legalize family violence and mistreatment of women.

The proposed law would make it illegal to question a relative of the accused as a witness to a crime. This would make it impossible for a woman to testify against her husband. A February 14, 2014, article at Human Rights Watch (HRW) quotes Brad Adams, Asia director of HRW, explaining that "should this law go into effect, Afghan women and girls will be deprived of legal protection from relatives who assault, forcibly marry, or even sell them." For example, as a February 11, 2014, article at CBS News explains, if the law were passed, it would be impossible to achieve justice in the case of Sahar Gul, a child bride whose in-laws "had kept her in a basement for six months after her arranged marriage, tortured her with hot irons, and ripped out her fingernails." The HRW article argues that President Hamid Karzai should refuse to sign the law in accord with the government's public stance in support of women's rights.

President Karzai did agree to alter the law, prompting relief among women's rights campaigners in and outside of Afghanistan. "Who says advocacy and lobbying does not work? It does and we have seen results!" said activist Samira Hamidi, as quoted by Emma Graham-Harrison in a February 17, 2014, article in the *Guardian*. However, Graham-Harrison says that the victory was mixed. Karzai appears to have allied himself broadly with factions who are working against women's rights, and even with Karzai's intervention, the law seems to reduce women's rights and makes it harder to prosecute domestic violence. The future of women's rights in Afghanistan, therefore, remains precarious and unclear.

The following chapter discusses women's rights and other human rights issues, including human rights abuses in government prisons and abuses by the Taliban.

"I burned my burqa when the Taliban left; I don't want a new one. I beg the US and the UK, do not leave us. Please stay. We are vulnerable, we are very afraid."

Western Presence Has Improved the Situation for Women in Afghanistan

Tracy McVeigh

Tracy McVeigh is chief reporter at the Observer. *In the following viewpoint, she says that the US and Western commitment to women's rights in Afghanistan has been limited and insufficient. However, she says that even the small gains women have made will be rolled back if the United States abandons Afghanistan as scheduled in 2014. She interviews a number of Afghan women who fear for their future after coalition forces leave the country and believe they will become a target for violence for their efforts to fight for women's rights.*

As you read, consider the following questions:

1. What does McVeigh say was the international community's great triumph in Afghanistan, and how is it being compromised?

2. Who is Fawzia Koofi, and how did Taliban rule affect her professionally?

3. What does Zarghona Walizada see as the one accomplishment that the Taliban cannot take away from her?

Pre-dawn in Kabul. In each dark street a short line of giant lightbulbs switch on, red, green and white, marking bakeries where warm slabs of golden flatbread are handed through open shop-front windows to sleepy little boys in white tunics and to men with blankets round their shoulders picking up lunch on their way to work.

Women's Bread and Men's Bread

"This is man's bread," says Hamil Fareed, a young baker. "Women's bread," he explains, is different, the dough kneaded at home by mothers and cooked out of sight at the back in the clay ovens and returned to the family.

The segregation of Kabul's daily bread is not a cultural tradition, but started under the [radical Islamic] Taliban in the 1990s. Faced with a half-starved city of war widows barred from working, studying or leaving their homes, someone began a clandestine communal fire pit where women could bake flatbread for their children and earn a few coins by selling them on. The UN [United Nations], impotent in quelling the vicious war, encouraged more such schemes and, when the Taliban soldiers who roamed the streets seemed to tolerate figures in burqas creeping out to little backstreet bakeries, heralded it as a "step forward" in women's rights.

The international community said the fall of the Taliban in 2001 [when the United States invaded Afghanistan] would bring in a new era of rights. Afghanistan's women and girls would be returned to schools and workplaces and freed from the infamously fierce restrictions on their lives. It was a key political justification used by the British and Americans for their continued presence. That year US secretary of state Colin Powell declared that restoring women's human rights would "not be negotiable." Prime minister Tony Blair promised: "The conflict will not be the end. We will not walk away, as the outside world has done so many times before." Now, with the withdrawal of international forces and their caravan of international agencies, consultants and contractors looming in 2014, there is evidence that Afghan women have seen very few of the promised changes and are terrified of the future.

The outside world has used Afghanistan as a pawn in its geopolitical "great games" since the 19th century and ensnared it in a labyrinth of strategic and economic interests. Since 2001 the country has received some £60bn of aid; there have been tangible improvements in education, maternal mortality, employment, and the representation of women in governance. But there are signs that those gains are too fragile to survive the international community's departure.

A 2012 survey of women across Afghanistan by the charity ActionAid found that nine out of 10 feared the departure of the international community, believing that their lives will significantly deteriorate. And violence against women has never been higher: 87% of women report domestic abuse.

Girls and Schooling

The return of 2.2 million girls to school after 2001 was considered the international community's great triumph, but in the past few years schools have been closing behind the departing backs of phased-out foreign forces. There have been reports of schoolgirls poisoned and beaten, head teachers assassinated and classrooms firebombed. The majority of girls don't stay on after fifth grade and nine out of 10 15-year-old girls are illiterate. Some girls are enrolled in schools but never go.

The British and other forces have built dozens of rural schools which the Afghan government cannot afford to keep open after 2014, and the same is true of the health clinics. Of the 5.8 million without access to health care in Afghanistan, 4.4 million are women.

There is rhetoric. And there is reality. Last year [2012] the UK's international development committee found "little evidence" to back up the British government's claims of commitment to promoting the rights of Afghan women. Among projects that receive the current £178m of UK annual aid poured into Afghanistan, only two are earmarked to help women.

The Elimination of Violence Against Women Act was brought into law in 2009, but it is widely ignored by courts; religious leaders have declared it un-Islamic; and in 2012 the US-backed government of President Hamid Karzai undermined it by upholding the right of a husband to beat his wife.

Half the female prison population are convicted of "moral crimes"—which include running away from violent husbands, fathers or in-laws. Federal law is universally ignored in the local courts, where nearly 90% of all criminal and civil legal disputes are settled, and where girls are bartered to settle family disputes and a man who kills his wife can expect a fine.

It is estimated the US government put $15m (£9.3m) into supporting the "informal justice" sector last year, entrenching repressive mentality. In April 2011, the Afghan government sought to reintroduce public morality laws, regulation was drafted to impose wedding codes to ensure that brides were modestly dressed, to ban music at weddings and to prevent male and female guests mixing. Shops were to be fined for selling inappropriate wedding clothes.

Fear of the Future

That caused consternation among the businessmen owners of Kabul's kitsch wedding halls. But Afghan's wealthy are unlikely to be around much longer. In the capital building grit still smothers the air, rising from spades and pickaxes as men work the giant ditches that line the pock-marked, uneven streets, but construction is slowing—many villas remain half-built and building sites deserted. The boom is over, the exodus has started, and property prices are dropping as houses empty of foreign agencies and wealthier Afghans.

Outside Kabul, in Balkh province where the Taliban is gaining strength, signs of its influence are everywhere. Few women in Mazar-i-Sharif travel without a burqa—last year the religious council of the famous Blue Mosque, one of the few places where women are able to socialise in public, banned women from its weekly meetings.

The women I spoke to in Afghanistan were deeply afraid of the future, and thoroughly exhausted by their precarious lives, in which bombs and rockets still explode. 2014 will bring elections and a powerful network of conservative men; Taliban and warlords are edging into the gap the internationals will leave. And the little clay ovens still cook up women's bread and men's bread in a country expecting their return. . . .

The MP: Fawzia Koofi

A mother of two teenage daughters, Fawzia Koofi, 36, has been MP [member of the Parliament] for Badakhshan province for seven years, and recently announced her intention to stand as a presidential candidate in 2014. Her husband died in a Taliban prison. Her father was killed by mujahedeen during the civil war. The seventh daughter, as a newborn she was left out in the sun to die before her parents relented.

If it hadn't been for the Taliban, Koofi would be a doctor now. "I was studying medicine when the Taliban came in 1996. That was my last day as a student. All of a sudden I was at home. You can see everything from your window, but you can't taste it, you can't touch it. I felt like a dead body."

Today she fears for the security of women in the public eye. "When the opportunity came in 2001, that was the time many of us started thinking of doing greater things, to contribute. We started programmes in health and education. We were told the international community was behind us—it was as if life had begun again after having been buried away in a box for so long.

"But the reality has not been what we were promised. There is lip service paid by the Afghan and US governments—gender projects created—but we can't access budgets.

"A few in this nation have come to the understanding that stopping girls' education halts a family's progress. I'm hopeful we will not go back to scratch. But I also know we will suffer—the main victims of the political games will be women and children."

She believes the women of Afghanistan have become "stronger" and adds: "They know how to use social networks, and if a woman is beaten in the streets then I hope there will be a phone camera and the world will know." But for women activists, "day by day it becomes more difficult. How many women really make their voices heard? I can count them on my fingers. There are 18 committees in our parliament, and I'm the only woman chair.

"When we talk about rights, about the taboos we face, they undermine you. Then they will use all the techniques including commenting—men will comment on your clothes, the way you talk and look, to bring you down."

The Doctor: Qumar Frahmand

Dr Qumar Frahmand, 40, is the head of a busy public clinic for women and children in Balkh province. She sees 35 to 40 patients a day. "The situation has been getting better all the time because of the international NGOs [nongovernmental organizations] coming in, and access to family planning, and vaccination for children has improved. But we still have a big problem with malnutrition because of poverty and ignorance.

"In the past 10 years, women have started to come out of their houses and see that having fewer children could mean a better life. Before, if a woman didn't have a boy she would keep having babies until she did.

"But will it all slip back? There is so much uncertainty, insecurity and rising unemployment, and the big thing I'm seeing is a rise in domestic violence. Last week a woman who

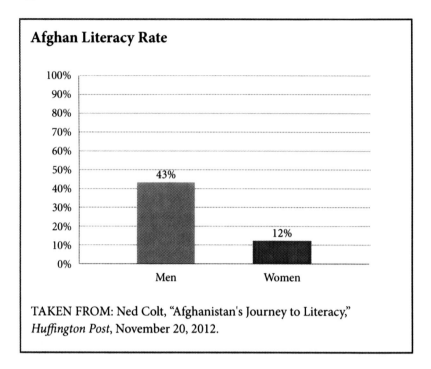

Afghan Literacy Rate

TAKEN FROM: Ned Colt, "Afghanistan's Journey to Literacy," *Huffington Post*, November 20, 2012.

was five months pregnant came here very seriously beaten and the foetus died. She went back to this husband because she has no other opportunity.

"We worry where we will find the money to keep the clinic going when the troops leave, and I cannot think what will happen if these clinic doors have to close. It's too terrible to think about. The security situation is worse for women in the rural areas and if they cannot come here ... I'm terrified to think how their lives will be."

The Businesswoman: Zarghona Walizada

A large desk puts space between Zarghona Walizada and her visitors. Beneath her chair are two large stones, her second line of defence. "I keep them close to my hands," she says. Her office in a suburb of Kabul—where she runs her own freight firm—is no longer a safe place.

"They came in cars with windows blacked out," she says. "My assistant tried to lock the doors, but these men with scarves around their faces came up the stairs with guns and broke down the door. I sat here behind my desk and stayed calm. I offered them tea, but I had my stones ready.

"They threatened me and demanded why I was not at home. For a long time we argued. They said it was not right for a woman to run a company. I thought they might shoot me, but finally they left. They'll be back."

On the wall is a newspaper cutting, a report of a speech by a UN official citing Walizada as an example of how women are forging ahead in Afghanistan. But Walizada is not the rule—she is the exception. "Women are encouraged by the US and the UN and the UK to make handicrafts, not to make business. The US army has contracts but gives them only to the corrupt politicians."

A widow, she trusts no one but "my driver, my brother and my sister. That is all. I can't worry about what people think. In Afghanistan two people accept me and 20 don't. People say bad things, Even the young boys make threats and throw stones."

She fears troop withdrawal in 2014 will kill the firm she has built. Her truck drivers face increasing threats from bandits, and three have been murdered in as many years. Fuel prices are rising, and those firms with US and UN contracts, which will dry up after the withdrawal, will come looking for the smaller freight contracts, like those she holds. "But I have my son studying in Paris, and at least I have done that—educated my son."

The Family: Maryam, Mahaba and Shahla Farid

Medical student Maryam Farid, 20, lost her voice after being caught up in a bomb blast aged six and still has a speech impediment. Her father, a university professor, is liberal in allowing his seven daughters to be educated—their mother ran an underground girls' school in their tiny flat during the Taliban rule—but he has chosen her future specialisation, gynaecology, so she will only work among females.

"Is it what I want to do?" asks Farid. "Maybe not. But there is no choice, and I have accepted that." Farid studies hard and looks tired. She shares a laptop with her sisters, but Internet access is prohibitively expensive for most young Afghans and the computer is mostly used to play educational CDs.

"The boys my age are the worst—they think we should not be studying," she says. "They say: what is the point, because after 2014 we will have to go back into the home again. They say it is against Islam. I know it is not. I love Islam. I am proud of my religion.

"All the girls are worried—we all think about this issue all the time, that after 2014 there will be no girl students and the women who worked to help other women in society will be killed.

"When I go to classes, only half of my energy is spent on my studies because the other 50% is spent in dealing with harassment from the male students. The teachers do not interfere because they do not want to get involved. You cannot complain to the principal because they say there are not these problems at our university, and I often want to leave. I am so tired of it."

Farid's mother, Shahla, is a former judge and teaches in the faculty of law and political science at Kabul University. She has acted as an advocate for battered women and is writing a book about women's rights in Afghanistan. A fifth of her students are female. She was the first woman from her region, Faryab province, to study law.

"At that time there were more girls studying than now," she tells me.

"Myself, I am afraid for 2014. I have seven daughters—two are married, five are studying. I fear my youngest two will not get the chance to go to university even though both are best in their class. The youngest, Mahaba, doesn't understand, but my 13-year-old feels hopeless about the situation."

She says that when the foreigners go, Afghan men will fight again. "Our government doesn't think about women. If I had known this would happen I would have taken another path and not have been an activist. So I'm angry. I am afraid for my daughters, who might be kidnapped or punished for the advocacy work I have done.

"Women have started to reduce our activities, because the closer we get to 2014 the laws made to support women are losing their strength. My students who can leave are doing so.

"I've a daughter who begs us every day to leave, but my husband will not. He says we must all love our country."

The Engineer: Raihana Karimi

Raihana Karimi is an engineer, like her husband. "But in this country it is shameful for a man to know a colleague's wife's name, so he could not have me working with him. He is happy now that I work among women."

In 2008 she joined a programme that trained women as paralegals. Now she runs a safe house for women, directly funded by the US embassy in Mazar-i-Sharif. "It's usually girls escaping forced marriage or violence—if they run away they can be arrested and go straight to jail. The effects of war are plain, and women bear the brunt. I talk to families to see if anything can be done to help solve the problems and their girl can return. But often they are very angry—they want to find and burn down the safe house."

Karimi says she now faces "a lot of threats. I know I will not only lose my job but will be the first target after the international community pulls out in 2014. The safe house will close, and although some NGOs say they will stay, everyone is working separately—there is no one aim. Our government is weak.

"I burned my burqa when the Taliban left; I don't want a new one. I beg the US and the UK, do not leave us. Please stay. We are very vulnerable, we are very afraid."

The Teacher: Shekiba Azizi

A 28-year-old teacher in a boys' high school in Mazar-i-Sharif, Shekiba Azizi also has three children of her own. She feels that uncertainty is allowing a creeping conservatism to dominate women's lives once again in Afghanistan. "Most of the other teachers now wear a burqa. But I hate it. I cannot see out and it's very claustrophobic. To walk to the bus stop I have to pass some warlords' houses, and they have armed guards who shout at me and harass me, so now I have to take a taxi to work, which is expensive. I even have to carry a burqa in my hand-bag now—just in case," she says, showing me the blue swathe of nylon fabric in her bag.

"The international community has spent a lot of money in Afghanistan, they say, but I have seen no effect on poor people. Now that they are going, we have the right to know our own future. They have to be clear about what is going to happen to us—they owe us that."

The Government Adviser:
Dr Monisa Sherzada Hassan

Dr Monisa Sherzada Hassan, 53, answers the communal door to her small apartment block in Kabul. Two small boys in the street stop and gape. Her head is covered but her heels are high and her makeup liberal. "I am a woman, and in my own home I will allow myself to be a woman even if outside I am not allowed," she says, leading the way to her modest living room, where every surface is heavy with welcoming platters of nuts and dried fruits. She escaped the Taliban in 1994, fleeing over the mountains by donkey with her toddler daughter. Her son and daughter are studying medicine in Germany. Hassan returned in 2001, and sits on a government committee set up on the insistence of the NATO [North Atlantic Treaty Organization] coalition to look at peace and reconciliation.

"There are 70 members, and nine are women. The women have just a symbolic presence. By voting they get nothing—committees only have functions to hear, not be heard. For women it's not that they are not tough or capable, but that their position is not equal. I see progress if a man says: 'Hello, how are you?' Otherwise they see a woman and they look over her head.

"The younger women are the most broken and depressed. We try to show them we are with them, but they see no future. They are dependent financially on their families.

"If the US and UK wanted, they could eliminate the Taliban in two days. They brought them and they can get rid of them. Now they are trying to leave Afghanistan isolated.

"I don't understand why the foreign forces would leave now, because they just ensure that the next Afghan crisis will be bigger. Our young people have never lived without bloodshed, and the hunger of youth is a great weapon for fundamentalists.

"When the conservatives come back they will shoot all these women who have been fighting for justice. Any fundamentalist knows the addresses of those who speak out for women's rights. The international community should support and protect these women, but they just think about their own departure. These women think about what will happen when the doors of these embassies are closed in their faces and when nobody at all will think about them.

"I am lucky in that I've got a German passport and can leave when I want, but I would beg the British and the American politicians who promised so much: please make one page in Afghanistan's history a lighter one. Before it's too late."

"For most Afghan women life has stayed the same, and for a great number, life has gotten much worse."

Women's Rights in Afghanistan Depends on Where One Lives

Stuart Whatley

Stuart Whatley is the managing blog editor at the Huffington Post. *In the following viewpoint, he writes that while women's status in Afghanistan has improved in urban areas, it has not gotten better in rural areas, and in many cases, has even worsened. He says that aid dollars often do not reach Afghans and that development projects need to be done with local cooperation and control. He concludes that troops in Afghanistan sometimes make things worse for women, by encouraging men to put even tighter strictures on their wives in reaction to the presence of foreign troops.*

As you read, consider the following questions:

1. Why is a women's dorm at Nangarhar University a necessity for women?

2. What does Ann Jones mean when she says that most US aid to Afghanistan is "phantom"?

3. According to Jones, what would Afghans have done differently if they had been in control of aid dollars in terms of school building?

In President Barack Obama's address to the Muslim world from Cairo, he spoke out against the subjugation of women and conveyed his belief that "a woman who is denied an education is denied equality." The speech comes two months after the [Afghan president Hamid] Karzai government was forced by international obloquy to rescind a controversial law that would have all but legalized rape within Shia [a Muslim denomination] marriages. And just one month after 90 Afghan teenage girls were hospitalized by a poison gas attack as punishment for their enrollment in school—the third such attack in as many weeks.

Cities vs. Rural Areas

Starkly disparate appraisals of the conditions for women in Afghanistan continue to paint what is, at best, a rather blurry picture. Determining whether the overall situation has improved since the [Islamic militant] Taliban was ousted in late 2001 can be difficult. And, as demonstrated by reports from sources who have recently returned from the war-ridden country, this determination is no less intractable now than in the past.

The primary reason is that conditions in Afghanistan are acutely compartmentalized into what is, in some regions, a muddling patchwork. Reports from one tribal village can be bright and optimistic while another locale only a few miles away will be rife with atrocities towards women and girls. "Problems in Afghanistan tend to be local in nature, not nationwide," says Stephen Brown, a humanitarian aid worker with the La Jolla Golden Triangle Rotary Club in San Diego, California, who has been in and out of both Pakistan and Afghanistan since 2002.

For his part, Brown sees the situation for women in Afghanistan as being wildly better overall than in 2002. He has spent the past months assisting his Rotary Club colleague Fary Moini in opening the first women's dormitory at Nangarhar University in Jalalabad. The idea is to bypass the requirement that women be accompanied by a male family member if they commute (which they all must, as there is never on-campus housing). Moini, like Brown, has worked intermittently in Afghanistan—in Kabul and Jalalabad, and in a number of smaller villages, including Surkhrood, Barabad and Laghman—and she supports his claim that conditions for women are markedly improved.

However, the fact that most of Moini and Brown's work has been in the more developed Jalalabad area may account for their rosy outlook. "Jalalabad is totally different. It's a prosperous town, and more secure," says Fahima Vorgetts of Women for Afghan Women, who runs women's shelters in Afghanistan's more rural and treacherous areas. Overall, according to Vorgetts, "the cities are better, women can go to work and school . . . in rural areas though, things haven't changed."

According to the United States Agency for International Development (USAID), 80 percent of Afghanis earn their living through agriculture, in rural areas. Moreover, the Afghan urban population is generally overestimated, the United [Nations Food] and Agriculture Organization (FAO) concludes.

By Vorgetts' account, the prospects for Afghan women were thought to have improved in the years following the Taliban's fall, but hope quickly dissipated when the [George W.] Bush administration's priorities shifted to Iraq. The little aid directed towards Afghanistan in the following years was allocated to the military, leaving almost nothing for vital improvements in education and infrastructure, laments Vorgetts.

But, according to USAID, the number of children now enrolled in school has increased sixfold to 6 million children—one-third of whom are girls—since the Taliban's fall. Moini and Brown, who previously opened a coed elementary school in Jalalabad that now enrolls 2,000 students, tell a similar story of expansive improvement in women and girls' education.

Getting Worse

However, the same criticism that these gains are exclusively in urban areas reemerges. Ann Jones, a women's rights expert and author of *Kabul in Winter: Life Without Peace in Afghanistan*, spent four years in Afghanistan as a journalist and aid worker, from 2002 to 2006, and has more recently been involved with *Rethink Afghanistan*, filmmaker and activist Robert Greenwald's latest Brave New Films documentary. She applauds the successes in developing areas such as Jalalabad, and even notes improvements in some rural localities where nongovernmental organizations (NGO) such as Vorgetts' Women for Afghan Women and the National Solidarity Programme have a strong presence. But overall, she is less sanguine than Moini and Brown. "All the positive changes are still insufficient to produce something like critical momentum, and all could be reversed in a moment by laws such as the Shia family law Karzai was ready to implement until international pressure gave him pause," writes Jones in an email to the *Huffington Post*.

One often highlighted tangible improvement is that women's rights protections are now codified into law. The Constitution of Afghanistan, ratified in early 2004, explicitly guarantees "equal rights and duties before the law" between men and women. But according to Jones, "although there have been improvements on paper in the Constitution and international treaties, for most Afghan women life has stayed the same, and for a very great number, life has gotten much worse." She attributes much of the deterioration to misappropriated development aid, government corruption and to NATO's [North Atlantic Treaty Organization's] war with the Taliban that rages mostly in the countryside.

According to the State Department human rights report for 2008, violence and the unequal treatment towards women, rather than being the exclusive behavior of Taliban militants, actually runs rampant among Afghan police and security officials as well, including the wanton rape of women prisoners by male police. Moreover, "authorities imprisoned an unknown number of women for reporting crimes perpetrated against them or to serve as substitutes for their husbands or male relatives convicted of crimes," reports the State Department.

Jones' critiques of US government aid, and USAID in particular, are enumerated in *Kabul in Winter* and in a lengthy *Huffington Post* jeremiad tellingly titled 'The Afghan Scam: The Untold Story of Why the U.S. Is Bound to Fail in Afghanistan.' "Most of what we call 'American aid' is phantom aid anyway. Either it never exists, or it goes into the pockets of private American contractors and never leaves the US. It's been calculated that 86 cents of every American aid dollar never leaves the United States," Jones tells Greenwald in *Rethink Afghanistan.*

Amnesty International seems to corroborate Jones' negative appraisal of the situation in its 2009 report covering the period between January and December 2008. For one, it notes the number of Afghan women in government has decreased since the initial years of the Constitution of Afghanistan. And in 2008, it is estimated that 60–80 percent of marriages were forced, and that a large portion were with young girls. Moreover, "the year saw increased attacks on schools, the intimidation of teachers and female students primarily by the Taliban, and greater disruption of classes because of armed conflict. In areas controlled by the Afghan government, both health and education systems suffered from inadequate funding, lack of qualified professionals, and security problems," states the report.

Aid Needs to Reach People

Vorgetts echoes Jones' frustration, insisting that Women for Afghan Women "can do a lot with very little," if only more development aid dollars reached NGOs like hers in the more marginalized and war-ravaged rural areas in the south and east. There are an estimated 20 women's shelters in Afghanistan, which has a population of 32 million people, and five of these are located in Kabul. As Jones notes, the same problem with disproportionate clustering can be said for schools. "What would Afghans have done differently, if they'd been in charge? They'd have built much smaller schools, and a lot more of them, in places more convenient to children than to foreign construction crews."

For their part, Moini and Brown recognize the importance of involving Afghans in Afghan development by making "sure they know that it's their project, not yours," Moini explains. This is, in fact, the crucial element of what has proven to be the Rotarians' winning strategy. The Nangarhar University dorm was built with funds from a number of independent donors, and with the local community's full involvement. But most importantly, says Moini, it was an Afghan project, not an American one.

There is an advantage to operating in Jalalabad, which despite its propinquity to the Taliban-ridden Peshawar, Pakistan, border about 100 miles to the east, is a relative oasis of modernity. But Moini and Brown's successes, and the lessons they have learned operating amidst such powerful traditional elements—dominant even in Jalalabad to a degree—leave them with no doubt that the same can be achieved elsewhere.

Afghanistan Unveiled

The Asia Foundation funded a poignant project of the [AINA] Afghan Media and Cultural Center, which resulted in a film called *Afghanistan Unveiled.*

Fourteen young Afghan women were taught how to use video cameras and were trained as video journalists. The young women then journeyed to various parts of the country, urban and rural, to interview women. The resulting film was fascinating both for the documentary footage the girls got and for the dramatic story of the girls' own lives unfolding. The women's world recorded by these young women had been inaccessible to male filmmakers even in pre-Taliban times because Afghan families simply don't let male strangers into the private portions of their homes; so these lives had been unseen by any public, even in the liberal era. What's more, the young videographers had all come of age in Taliban times. They themselves had hardly ever set foot outside their own compounds and didn't know what the street looked like one block over from their own. Now they were having the revelatory adventure of a lifetime, traveling to places as far away as Herat, Mazar-i-Sharif, and Khost, talking to strangers, finding out about their fellow Afghans, and in the process—it's plain from their commentary—finding out about themselves.

Tamim Ansary, Games Without Rules:
The Often Interrupted History of Afghanistan.
Philadelphia, PA: Public Affairs, 2012, pp. 284–285.

By contrast, it is no surprise that those who have seen Afghanistan's most destitute corners have their doubts about the situation for women. At one point in *Rethink Afghanistan*, Greenwald visits a refugee camp of mostly widows who are so deprived of basic needs that they must sell their own daughters to survive. Those who visit these places and then return to the developed areas around Kabul, Jalalabad, Mazar-i-Sharif or Herat describe two vastly different worlds.

To many, the differences appear insurmountable because of what is often described as the entrenched tribal culture prevalent in rural areas. But Vorgetts, who grew up in Afghanistan and remembers far better conditions for women just 30 years ago, promptly dismisses this argument. "It means it's not culture, it's forced by the fundamentalists," she says, adding that she believes education to be the most powerful weapon against these "root causes of terrorism."

Troops Do Not Help

The disparate reports out of Afghanistan suggest that the polarity of conditions between urban and rural areas is increasing. However, improvements in the former could lead the way for improvements in the latter by, if nothing else, demonstrating that improvement is indeed possible. But a key issue is the war. President Obama is shifting the US focus from Iraq back to Afghanistan with the deployment of 21,000 additional troops and a $96.7 billion bill that passed the House in mid-May. Yet many involved in humanitarian and development aid bemoan the troop increase, such as Vorgetts, who points out that the presence of NATO soldiers in villages gives men even more reason to sequester women indoors, while instituting oppressive behavioral and dress standards.

Likewise, Dr. Roshanak Wardak, one of the Afghan Parliament's few women members, tells Greenwald in *Rethink Afghanistan* that there are far better ways to improve the situation than fighting. She insists that a political solution exists to accommodate hard-line elements into the parliament that will spur a productive quid pro quo, with each side accepting certain conditions from the other, including respect for women.

But the Obama administration's troop increase and its replacement of General David McKiernan with counterinsurgency specialist Lt. General Stanley McChrystal indicates that the US will continue prosecuting the war in Afghanistan certainly for the immediate future. The most aid groups can hope for—especially for women—is better disbursement channels for development dollars entering Afghanistan. And in the meantime, the activists and aid workers have no intention of relinquishing their efforts.

| "It defies reason to call for international troops to remain even longer as a solution to the problem they have exacerbated."

US Presence Has Hurt Women in Afghanistan

Bretigne Shaffer

Bretigne Shaffer is a journalist and writer. In the following viewpoint, she argues that conditions for women in Afghanistan are actually worse under the occupation than they were during the time of the Taliban. Most women have no more rights than in the past, and they also face the dangers that come from war and conflict. The war has also empowered many fundamentalist factions, she says. She concludes that Western forces should leave Afghanistan, and she rejects the argument that they will help women if they remain.

As you read, consider the following questions:

1. What publications does Shaffer say have been discussing the plight of Afghan women?

2. According to Sonali Kohatkar, how has violence against women increased under the occupation?

3. How does the CIA use Afghan women as propaganda, according to Shaffer?

The plight of Afghan women is in the news again. In December [2013] Reuters warned that "(a)larm rises for Afghan women prisoners after Western troops leave", and *MacLean's* published a plea from Afghan parliamentarian and women's rights advocate Fawzia Koofi, for Western troops to remain in her country. Earlier this month, Russia Today reported that:

> "Violent crimes against women in Afghanistan reached an unprecedented level of brutality in 2013, an Afghan human rights watchdog has announced as the US-led coalition prepares to withdraw.

> "Chair of the Afghanistan Independent Human Rights Commission (AIHRC), Sima Samar, told Reuters that the pace and the hideousness of attacks on women intensified in 2013 with a 25 per cent surge in cases from March through September.

> "'The brutality of the cases is really bad. Cutting the nose, lips and ears. Committing public rape," Samar said. "Mass rape. . . . It's against dignity, against humanity.'

> "The spokeswoman noted that as the withdrawal deadline draws near for international troops, women in tribal areas are less protected, leaving them vulnerable to violent assaults.

> "'The presence of the international community and provincial reconstruction teams in most of the provinces was giving people confidence,' Samar said. 'There were people there trying to protect women. And that is not there anymore, unfortunately.'"

The implication here, of course, is that the "international" (read: occupying) troops in Afghanistan were somehow protecting women from the brutality being inflicted upon them, and that with their departure Afghan women will be left vulnerable to further assault.

Troops Do Not Help

Had the writer bothered to put the current brutality into context though, it would have been clear that the reality is something very, very different. As I wrote in 2010, the US-led invasion and occupation of Afghanistan has only made things worse for the women who live there:

"Says Ann Jones, journalist and author of *Kabul in Winter*, 'For most Afghan women, life [since the occupation] has stayed the same. And for a great number, life has gotten much worse.'

"Sonali Kolhatkar, codirector of the Afghan Women's Mission, says 'the attacks against women both external and within the family have gone up. Domestic violence has increased. (The current) judiciary is imprisoning more women than ever before in Afghanistan. And they are imprisoning them for running away from their homes, for refusing to marry the man that their family picked for them, for even being a victim of rape.'

"Anand Gopal, Afghanistan correspondent for the *Wall Street Journal*, says 'The situation for women in the Pashtun area is actually worse than it was during the Taliban time. . . . (U)nder the Taliban, women were kept in burqas and in their homes, away from education. Today, the same situation persists. They're kept in burqas, in homes, away from education, but on top of that they are also living in a war zone.'

"'Five years after the fall of the Taliban, and the liberation of women hailed by [American First Lady] Laura Bush and Cherie Blair [the wife of former British prime minister Tony Blair], thanks to the US and British invasion,' wrote the *Independent*'s Kim Sengupta in November of 2006, 'such has been the alarming rise in suicide that a conference was held on the problem in the Afghan capital just a few days ago.'"

When I wrote this piece in 2010, there seemed to be a concerted campaign in the media to use the plight of Afghan women as a rallying cry against ending the US occupation at that time. By sheer coincidence, a leaked CIA [Central Intelligence Agency] memorandum from March of 2010 ("CIA Red Cell Special Memorandum: Afghanistan: Sustaining West European Support for the NATO-led Mission—Why Counting on Apathy Might Not Be Enough") had outlined "possible PR strategies to shore up public support in Germany and France for a continued war in Afghanistan."

According to the memo:

"The proposed PR strategies focus on pressure points that have been identified within these countries. For France it is the sympathy of the public for Afghan refugees and women.... Outreach initiatives that create media opportunities for Afghan women to share their stories with French, German, and other European women could help to overcome pervasive skepticism among women in Western Europe toward the ISAF [International Security Assistance Force] mission.... Media events that feature testimonials by Afghan women would probably be most effective if broadcast on programs that have large and disproportionately female audiences."

Conditions for women in Afghanistan have badly deteriorated under the US-led occupation, and they continue to deteriorate under a foreign occupation that only strengthens local fundamentalist leadership. It defies reason to call for international troops to remain even longer as a solution to the problem they have exacerbated.

▌ *"We just let them live with the fear."*

Drone Strikes Are an Unethical Violation of Human Rights

Conor Friedersdorf

Conor Friedersdorf is a staff writer at the Atlantic, *where he focuses on politics and national affairs. In the following viewpoint, he argues that drone attacks by the United States in places like Afghanistan, Pakistan, and Yemen are unethical and immoral. He says that the drone attacks spread fear among innocent civilians. He also argues that the Barack Obama administration refuses to be transparent about the strikes and fails to admit errors or to compensate victims. He also says that drone strikes create a dangerous precedent in normalizing drones, which could one day be used in other conflicts by other actors.*

As you read, consider the following questions:

1. What does Friedersdorf list as three troubling implications of drones?

2. How does Friedersdorf say drones might be a threat to America in the long term?

Conor Friedersdorf, "Distant Death the Case for a Moratorium on Drone Strikes," *Atlantic*, November 14, 2013. © 2013 The Atlantic Media Co., as first published in The Atlantic Magazine. All rights reserved. Distributed by Tribune Content Agency, LLC.

3. What is wrong with the Obama administration's leaking classified information, according to Friedersdorf?

What if I told you all that an armed Predator drone is circling above us right now? It isn't. So don't worry. But if an armed drone was there, would it make you feel anxious? If we could hear the buzz of its engine, would that change the tenor of our time together? Now let's imagine that this drone is hovering overhead because there's a terrorist hanging out 100 yards away from this building. We're often told how precise drone strikes are. [Barack] Obama administration officials have called them surgical. If a surgery were happening in the building next door I wouldn't be worried about getting nicked by the scalpel.

Would you be worried for your safety if you were 100 yards away from a drone strike? Say you're laying in bed one night, and in the house next door, a terrorist is laying in his bed.

Would you want a drone strike to take him out?

If next door is too close for comfort, do you think the U.S. military or the CIA [Central Intelligence Agency] should be allowed to carry out drone strikes on terrorists with innocent people next door? . . .

Targeted Killings

Soon, I hope debates on the merits of targeted killing are taking place not only at universities, but inside the federal court system. The Obama administration hopes to avoid that fate. Its lawyers would have us believe that targeted killing with drones is a state secret, or else a so-called political question that isn't properly decided by judges.

In Israel, a state with national security challenges far greater than ours, the Supreme Court grappled with this same question. Do judges have any role to play in targeted killing? They didn't see it as a close question. They saw their role as determining "the permissible and the forbidden" in combat that implicates "the most basic right of a human being—the right to life." They affirmed that "non-justiciability cannot prevent the examination of that question." I suspect [Founding Father] James Madison would find their approach more prudent than what the Obama administration suggests. The administration would have us believe not only that they're empowered to kill an American in secret, but that after the fact, courts should refrain from judging whether the killing violated the right to life of the target.

Does anyone else think that's a recipe for abuses?

But legal doctrine is not my area of expertise. So I'd like to begin, instead, with a moral question: Is it ever okay for the U.S. to kill people with drones? "This is actually an easy question," Mr. [Benjamin Wittes] once said, "since drones clearly enable more discriminating and deliberative targeting than do alternative weapon systems." I want to repeat that. He thinks that once you've decided to use force, drones could be the most moral choice, because they're more deliberative and discriminating.

That's an interesting standard.

It got me thinking: Is it ever okay for the U.S. to use biological weapons? Is *that* ever the most moral option? They're terrifying. A taboo surrounds them, and treaties prohibit their use.

And yet.

Imagine a remote al-Qaeda [terrorist group] compound. Inside its walls are a few dozen adult bomb makers, their wives, and many scores of children. Explosives are everywhere. A drone strike or a firefight would cause the whole place to blow. But a U.S. scientist has an alternative: a biological agent that, if dispersed over the compound, would target, incapacitate and kill only the adult males. Only the militants—no one else.

Would that discriminating bioweapon be the most moral option?

That's a hard question. On one hand, maybe you save a lot of innocent women and children. On the other hand, using a bioweapon would have implications that transcend any one discrete mission. Similarly, using weaponized drones has implications that go far beyond any one discrete strike. Let's think through some of them.

The Implications of Drones

1) For a drone strike to be an option, the United States has to fund a drone industry to build its arsenal, negotiate leases for drone bases in various foreign countries—often non-democracies where the people do not want a drone base and would vote against it if they were afforded rights that we think of as universal. In building this drone fleet and the infrastructure to use it, America inevitably normalizes the notion of weaponized drones all over the globe, and it seeds an industry that is certain to contribute to the weapon's proliferation in the future.

2) In thought experiments, we may be able to separate the questions, "Should force be used?" and, "If so, what is the most ethical weapon available?" But the questions are not typically asked independent of one another. A fleet of drones at the ready significantly lowers the costs of certain lethal operations. As we've seen, it also makes perpetual war possible in a way that it wasn't before. Due to drones, lethal acts occur that wouldn't have happened in a world without drones. And those acts can be carried out with more secrecy than would otherwise be possible.

3) The ability to hover for hours or even days does permit deliberation and discrimination. But hovering also imposes a cost on many thousands of innocents. Drones don't just affect targets, actual and aborted. They affect whole communities. People who live in communities where drones hover overhead report severe anxiety, terrified children, mental health prob-

lems, trouble sleeping, paranoia (and after drone strikes occur, pervasive mistrust as people wonder if a local helped call down the Hellfire missile). Communities stop gathering in large numbers to attend prayers or public meetings. They're forced to live in what any of us might consider a dystopia, if we were forced to live there. How would you feel if every night you had to tuck your children into bed as the buzz of drones overhead made them afraid that they'd never wake up again?

As it turns out, asking if there's ever a discrete targeted killing where a drone is the most ethical option tells us very little. Like land mines or bioweapons or torture to prevent a nuclear holocaust, a drone strike might be the most ethical option in a given situation. But a blanket ban might nevertheless be an ethical imperative. Perhaps so many terrible consequences inevitably flow from building, maintaining and using a fleet of armed drones that a ban leaves us better off.

The better question is, "Can maintaining *a drone strike program* ever be ethical?"

To me, that is a very tough question. Since my time is limited, I want to focus on a related question that is far more urgent: Is America's actual drone strike program ethical?

That's an easier question. It is not ethical.

No Responsibility

What's least defensible is how we respond after killing innocents, presumably by accident. The moral thing would be to acknowledge responsibility; to apologize; to explain how it happened, and what steps are being taken to prevent the same mistake; and to compensate the victims. Our typical response is more like what you'd expect from a hit-and-run driver. We take no responsibility. We offer no explanation. If steps are taken to prevent the same mistake from recurring, they are taken in secret, and without the benefit of independent, disinterested reformers.

Worst of all, innocents with limbs blown off are left to fend for themselves; impoverished families are left to bear the costs of burying their dead and repairing their homes. Survivors, who have no idea why their loved one was killed, can't help but fear they'll be next, and the U.S. does nothing to reassure them.

We just let them live with the fear.

There are also numerous reports that the U.S. carries out so-called double-tap drone strikes, where we fire a missile at someone, then fire another at rescuers who rush to the scene or mourners who attend a funeral. Of course, it could be the case that a rescuer, or a funeral attendee, is also a terrorist. But by carrying out these strikes, we prevent rescuers from rushing to the scene even when innocents are hit.

Finally, there is a question of proportionality. Drone strikes are a response to a real threat. Terrorists are bent on attacking us. At the same time, terrorist attacks are relatively rare. Terrorist attacks perpetrated by people in Yemen, as opposed to homegrown threats like Tim McVeigh or the Tsarnaev brothers,[1] are more rare still. Are all the people, including innocents, that we've killed in, say, Yemen really a proportionate response to the threat that we face from terrorists there?

I'd say that is far from clear.

The Obama administration says it only takes lethal action when the target poses "an imminent threat of violent attack." It is absurd to suggest the thousands we've killed were all imminent threats. I suspect that the actual standard is hidden because it is indefensible.

Legitimizing Drones

If our drone program is immoral, does it at least keep us safer? The Obama administration says so. But there is nothing resembling hard evidence to suggest that they are right. I trust

---

1. Tim McVeigh blew up a federal building in Oklahoma City in 1995. The Tsarnaev brothers planted explosives at the Boston Marathon in 2013.

Drone Mistake

One day while her father was out selling candies, Roya and her two sisters were trudging home carrying buckets of water. Suddenly, they heard a terrifying whir and then there was an explosion: something terrible had dropped from the sky, tearing their house apart and sending the body parts of their mother and two brothers flying through the air.

The Americans must have thought Roya's home was part of a nearby Taliban housing compound. In the cold vernacular of military-speak, her family had become "collateral damage" in America's war on terror.

When Roya's father came home, he carefully collected all the bits and pieces of his pulverized family that he could find, buried them immediately according to Islamic tradition, and then sank into a severe state of shock.

Roya became the head of her household. She bundled up her surviving sisters, grabbed her father, and fled. With no money or provisions, they trekked through the Hindu Kush [mountains], across the Khyber Pass, and into Pakistan.

Medea Benjamin,
Drone Warfare: Killing by Remote Control.
New York: OR Books, 2012, p. 2.

you're all familiar with the argument that we are creating more terrorists than we are killing. Al-Qaeda certainly uses our drone strikes as a recruiting tool. Faisal Shahzad, who attempted to bomb Times Square, spoke in court about "the drone strikes in Somalia and Yemen and in Pakistan."

At the very least, drone strikes fuel anti-Americanism. And we have reason to worry that President Obama isn't as attuned to blowback from drone strikes as he ought to be. Presidents have a perverse incentive to focus too much on keeping us safe through the end of a four-year term, and too little on keeping us safe in the long run.

In the long run, it isn't just blowback that we ought to worry about. There's a strong case to be made that Americans are being shortsighted about drones themselves. Our military is the strongest in the world. The gap between our Air Force and the next best is huge. In the short term, our near monopoly on drones has given us an even bigger advantage. But these are naturally asymmetric weapons. Cheap. Far easier to build and operate than a fighter jet. Relatively inconspicuous. As they spread to other states and non-state actors, they'll decrease our edge. Perhaps we should've used this window, where we're the undisputed leader on drones, to shape international norms more to our long-term advantage.

Instead, we've set precedents that we'd hate to see other countries adopt. As we legitimate drone warfare, we legitimate it for everyone. Does anyone else find that scary?

This shortsightedness raises a larger question that isn't often asked in the drone debate. How competent and trustworthy is America's national security leadership? That seems like a relevant variable. If the people in charge enjoy a deserved reputation for prudence and moral behavior in waging the war on terrorism, we might be more inclined to permit them a tool like drones that significantly lowers the cost of killing people. On the other hand, if our national security bureaucracy often acts imprudently, immorally, or unlawfully, we might be more inclined, as citizens, to deny them this tool, or at least to subject it to strict oversight.

What I see is a national security state undeserving of our trust. It failed to prevent the September 11 [2001, also referred to as 9/11] terrorist attacks; misrepresented the threat posed by Iraq; invaded that country with insufficient planning; presided over the abuse of detainees at Abu Ghraib [in Iraq] and

Guantánamo Bay [Gitmo, in Cuba]; initiated an official program of torture; broke the law with warrantless spying on Americans; lost the trove of WikiLeaks documents; then lost the trove of [Edward] Snowden documents.[2] And after all of these failures of competence and character, we're supposed to trust the CIA and the Pentagon to get good intelligence prior to drone strikes; to follow the law; to act morally in a way that neither stains our national honor nor needlessly creates enemies?

And to do it all in secret?

We're supposed to trust the CIA, with its very recent history of torture and illegally destroying evidence of torture, to run a secret killing program that adequately safeguards innocents? We're supposed to trust a government that threw many innocents and low-level offenders into prison at Gitmo, telling us they were all the worst of the worst, to direct drone strikes only at the worst of the worst?

Why would we trust them to do that?

Administration Lies

And there is so much particular to our drone strike program that should deepen our mistrust. For example: The Obama administration's decision to treat targeted killing with drones as a state secret, except when it wanted to brag about a kill; a definition of militants that encompassed all men of military age we happened to kill; the many officials who've lied about the number of innocents killed in drone strikes; the Obama administration's alarming notion that it is empowered to secretly order the extrajudicial drone killings of American citizens, even if they're not on any battlefield; and the killing of [Islamic militant] Anwar al-Awlaki's 16-year-old son [Abdulrahman al-Awlaki]. In that case, a presumably innocent teen-

2. Classified documents were leaked to WikiLeaks in 2010. Edward Snowden leaked documents about US surveillance in 2013.

ager was killed; though an American citizen, the government has offered no explanation for his death.

I'd like to read you a short passage from the book *Dirty Wars* by Jeremy Scahill, who has done on-the-ground reporting on drone strikes in Yemen:

> A former senior official in the Obama administration told me that after Abdulrahman's killing, the president was "surprised and upset and wanted an explanation." The former official, who worked on the targeted killing program, said that according to intelligence and Special Operations officials, the target of the strike was [Ibrahim] al-Banna, the al Qaeda in the Arabian peninsula propagandist. "We had no idea the kid was there. We were told al-Banna was alone," the former official told me. Once it became clear that the teenager had been killed, he added, military and intelligence officials asserted, "It was a mistake, a bad mistake."

> However, John Brennan, at the time President Obama's senior adviser on counterterrorism and homeland security, "suspected that the kid had been killed intentionally and ordered a review. I don't know what happened with the review."

So an American kid is killed. The president has no idea why. At best, a drone strike was ordered on faulty intelligence. At worst, the kid was killed deliberately.

Even John Brennan, Obama's chief counterterrorism officer, apparently found it plausible that there was something untoward about the killing. He reportedly conducted a review. But the whole episode remains cloaked in secrecy, as if American national security depends on our not knowing the truth about why a 16-year-old kid was killed. Is there any more clear example of self-serving secrecy? And this story has only garnered attention because an American kid was involved. How many innocent 16-year-old Pakistanis or Yemenis have we killed?

The national security state has taken steps to make sure that we don't find out. The same people implicated in killing hundreds of innocents, whether negligently or intentionally, are the ones who decide what the public will and won't be told. Again, that's a recipe for corruption. Also objectionable is the Obama administration's habit of treating various matters as classified, then authorizing leaks so that they can get out their story anonymously, without the degree of accountability that would come from an official putting their name behind it. If something can be discussed in an authorized leak, it can be declassified.

On the subject of transparency, Robert Chesney points out that the Obama administration has openly explained its belief that the authorization for use of military force passed after 9/11 authorizes it to kill not just al Qaeda members, but "associated forces." (I wonder, by the way, whether members of Congress understood themselves to be approving many drone strikes in Yemen 11 years later.) Anyway, Chesney goes on to point out that "the administration has resisted public disclosure of which groups come within the scope of that understanding, and has not made clear what factors suffice to make a group an associated force."

He adds that "for that matter, it has not been particularly forthcoming on these issues with Congress." Is this permissible? An administration that isn't even transparent about who the enemy is in a war that it's waging? That seems absurd. . . .

Need to Know

I'd suggest that, if we don't know what went wrong, or why, or how we can minimize the chances of similar disasters—and if, in general, we worry that our drone strike program isn't transparent enough, which is to say, that it is more vulnerable to abuses than it ought to be—if we believe that, it is our responsibility to call for a moratorium on drone strikes. They should stop at least until they are made as transparent as they ought to be, and until we know what goes wrong, why and how to fix it. That's what you do when a program induces nausea.

You call for it to stop.

But many who happily concede various flaws in the drone program won't go so far as to call on the Obama administration to halt it, pending reforms that they agree are necessary.

Why?

> "To leave the militants alone is, at the very least, to invite attacks in Pakistan and around the world. . . . But to root them out through a ground campaign would kill and displace far more civilians than the use of drones would."

Drone Strikes Are an Ethical Response to Terrorism

David Aaronovitch

David Aaronovitch is a regular columnist for the Times *of London and the author of* Voodoo Histories: The Role of the Conspiracy Theory in Shaping Modern History. *In the following viewpoint, he argues that drone attacks are a relatively cheap and relatively safe way to target terrorists and insurgents. He says that Taliban and al Qaeda in Afghanistan and Pakistan would commit violence if not stopped, and he argues that drones result in fewer civilian casualties than a full-out ground attack would. He says that drone critics serve a valuable function by encouraging oversight, but he concludes that drones are ultimately effective and humane.*

As you read, consider the following questions:

1. To what does James Traub compare Obama's drone campaign?

2. What did the Taliban do in Swat, and why does Aaronovitch see this as an argument for drone attacks?

3. According to Aaronovitch, what is the attitude toward drones of those who live in the areas affected?

In real life magic does not charm us for long. Over the past decade the pilotless drone seemed like a genie's answer to a fervent rub of the lamp.

The [Barack] Obama administration in particular wanted something that would allow the US and its allies to destroy al-Qa'ida and other terrorist networks and permit some breathing space to allow it to get its troops out of Afghanistan while maintaining the elected government in place. It wanted some happy medium between pricey and bloody boots-on-the-ground nation-building on the one hand and dangerous fingers-in-the-ears lala-ing on the other.

Drones as Solution

The Americans rubbed the lamp and the Predator and the Reaper appeared. As the US withdrew from Iraq and first surged and then prepared to withdraw from Afghanistan, so the number of drone attacks, particularly in northwest Pakistan, increased. "Militant" bases and leaders ("terrorist" now being regarded as an unanalytical expression) have been pulverised in remote and perilous places without the loss of a single soldier or flier. And for remarkably little cost. Drones were the Heineken [a beer] of warfare.

But in the past year or so a voluble campaign of criticism has grown. The US commentator James Traub, not himself a critic of drones, put it succinctly in *Foreign Policy* magazine: "There is a real danger that . . . drone warfare will come to be seen as the dark arts of the Obama administration, as torture and 'rendition' were for President George W. Bush."

For the purpose of this important argument I will ignore the routine anti-Americans. Some of them will not be satisfied or convinced until they find themselves hanged publicly for blasphemy outside the Caliph's palace.

Rather I want to deal with those arguments that cause me—as someone inclined to sympathise with Obama's dilemmas—most difficulty. That's not to say that there isn't a tendency towards exaggeration among anti-dronites. The Bureau of Investigative Journalism, despite the *Newsnight* debacle [in which a BBC program made false accusations of sexual abuse], has done good work on the effects of drone strikes. Even so, to claim, as it has done, that "an occasional tactic has, over time, morphed into an industrialised killing process" is to tip analysis over into advocacy. As we shall see.

The Case Against Drones

Those who argue vociferously against drones make, in essence, four arguments. The first is that too many civilians are killed or traumatised. The second is that drone strikes fail to reduce armed militancy and may be counter-productive by causing radicalisation. The third is that they are either contrary to international law or create dangerous precedents. And the fourth—most subtle of all—is that their very cheapness removes an important inhibition in the use of extreme violence.

Any civilian death represents a person with a name and a grieving family. But if we imagine for a moment that action does have to be taken against those who would kill us if they could, then the possibility of innocent life being lost is always present. Especially when there are no uniforms or flags.

So one question is whether drones kill or wound more or fewer civilians than other forms of military action. Here, even by the bureau's figures for Pakistan of a maximum of 3400 deaths, it is conceded that somewhere between 400 and 900 were of civilians. Meaning, of course, that something between 2500 and 3000 were al-Qa'ida, foreign jihadis or [the Islamic militant] Taliban.

In 2007–08 the Pakistani government let the Pakistani Taliban take over the province of Swat, where Malala Yousafzai was at school. The idea seemed to be that local militants would be satisfied with their province and might, left to themselves, exercise restraint. They weren't and they didn't. They blew up schools, decapitated enemies in public in the marketplaces and allowed Swat to be used as a base for attacks on the Pakistani state. The Pakistani Army retook Swat in a campaign in which thousands died and hundreds of thousands were displaced.

To leave the militants alone is, at the very least, to invite attacks in Pakistan and around the world from bases in the borderlands. This isn't conjecture. But to root them out through a ground campaign would kill and displace far more civilians than the use of drones would.

So to the second argument. As far as I can see, the accuracy of drones and the sophistication of their warheads (allied to what appears to be an often reliable intelligence operation on the ground) has, according to the evidence, reduced the effectiveness and incidence of terrorist attacks in Pakistan and outside. Young jihadis from around the world can no longer regard attendance at a training camp in Waziristan as the safe bit before the big operation. Remarkably, in view of the arguments of the no-drone campaigners, those who actually live in the areas of drone strikes are less hostile to them than Pakistanis generally. Living with jihadis can be a pain.

So what about the law? With no actual declared belligerency between droners and dronees, doesn't the drone war amount to illegal state-sponsored assassination? And if we can do it, why shouldn't China, Russia and any old autocrat with a model airplane and a grenade?

This will be tested in the courts and it's right that it should be. My instinct is that the history of terrorist violence and its nature will show plenty of cause for most drone strikes. The precedent argument is an imponderable, but it should be said that two atomic bombs were dropped in 1945 and none have been since.

Drone Creep

Which leaves us with number four. And this is where I patronise the antis by saying that I'm glad they exist, even if I disagree with them. Because this point has truth to it. Drones are so easy, so cheap, so comparatively accurate, that we might well feel that we could use them in situations and in numbers we otherwise wouldn't contemplate. In other words, we might get drone creep. So let's keep an eye on it.

I am an interventionist and, resources permitting, in favour of nation-building. It's a view that is out of fashion for obvious reasons. But the consequence of this shift away from expensive direct intervention cannot be "do nothing". So it's very likely to be more drones.

Periodical and Internet Sources Bibliography

The following articles have been selected to supplement the diverse views presented in this chapter.

Shakeela Abrahimkhil	"UN Human Rights Chief Worried About Afghan Regress," TOLOnews.com, September 17, 2013.
BBC News Asia	"Sahar Gul: The Fears of a Tortured Afghan Child Bride," July 15, 2013.
Eve Conant	"Rollback of Women's Rights: Not Just in Afghanistan," *National Geographic*, February 20, 2014.
Megan Ferringer	"Razia Jan Fights to Educate Girls in Rural Afghanistan," *Christian Science Monitor*, March 19, 2014.
Emma Graham-Harrison	"New Afghanistan Law to Silence Victims of Violence Against Women," *Guardian*, February 4, 2014.
Ewen MacAskill and Owen Bowcott	"UN Report Calls for Independent Investigations of Drone Attacks," *Guardian*, March 10, 2014.
Alex Mihailovich	"Afghanistan's Big Steps Backward on Human Rights," Sun News Network, February 17, 2014.
Patrick Quinn	"Afghanistan Considering Re-Introducing Stoning as Punishment for Adultery, Human Rights Watch Says," *National Post* (Toronto), November 25, 2013.
Amanda Terkel	"Afghanistan Withdrawal Puts Programs for Women and Girls at Risk, Top Watchdog Warns," *Huffington Post*, October 29, 2013.
Dylan Welch	"Afghanistan Commitment to Human Rights Waning: U.N.," Reuters, September 17, 2013.

For Further Discussion

Chapter 1

1. Isaac Chotiner argues that the United States should not pursue diplomatic negotiations with the Taliban in light of the group's apparent reluctance to take such talks seriously. In your opinion, does the evidence Chotiner offers in relation to the Taliban's talks with Afghanistan and Pakistan justify this position? Why, or why not?

2. Ivan Eland contends that the United States should withdraw all of its remaining forces from Afghanistan as soon as possible. What reasons does he offer for taking this tactical course of action? Do you agree or disagree with Eland's argument? Explain.

3. Aaron Ellis suggests that Britain should resume its diplomatic relations with Iran to better facilitate the stabilization of Afghanistan. Why does he believe this approach would be more effective than continuing to harbor a hostile relationship with Iran? Do you think Ellis is correct? Why, or why not?

Chapter 2

1. According to Thomas H. Johnson, America's strategy for installing American-style democratic institutions in Afghanistan is fundamentally flawed and, therefore, doomed to failure. What does he think is wrong with this strategy? How might the American government alter its approach so as to have a better chance of success? Explain.

2. The Associated Press suggests that the rapid development of media in Afghanistan since the fall of the Taliban is a sign that efforts to establish democracy in that country are succeeding. How does the growth of media correlate with the spread of democracy? Explain.

3. In arguing his point that corruption within the ranks of the Afghan police force is beneficial for the Taliban, author Brian Brady quotes a report that describes such corruption as "endemic" in the region. What does the term "endemic" mean in this context, and how does that meaning play into Brady's argument?

Chapter 3

1. The Daily Bell contends that the West's persistence in democratizing Afghanistan is driven by a desire for control of the region and the establishment of Western financial institutions there, despite public statements suggesting that the war is being fought over resources. What evidence does the author offer to support this hypothesis? Do you agree with the author's position? Why, or why not?

2. J. Alexander Thier argues that the significant progress the Afghan economy has made since the fall of the Taliban is positively indicative of the country's ability to continue developing after the US withdrawal in 2014. In your opinion, does Thier provide sufficient evidence to support his position? Why, or why not?

3. Gopal Ratnam's report predominantly suggests that the Afghan economy is likely to decline when Western forces begin their withdrawal at the end of 2014 and that such economic circumstances may facilitate Taliban resurgence. Do you agree with this assessment? Explain your reasoning.

Chapter 4

1. Bretigne Shaffer contends that media reports suggesting violence against Afghan women has increased as a result of the anticipated troop withdrawal are inaccurate in that such violence has been a consistent problem throughout the duration of the foreign occupation. Do you agree with her position? Why, or why not?

2. Conor Friedersdorf argues that the use of drone strikes is an unethical and potentially dangerous means of waging war. David Aaronovitch argues that drone strikes offer an effective, efficient method for fighting terrorists and insurgents. With which author do you agree, and why?

Organizations to Contact

The editors have compiled the following list of organizations concerned with the issues debated in this book. The descriptions are derived from materials provided by the organizations. All have publications or information available for interested readers. The list was compiled on the date of publication of the present volume; the information provided here may change. Be aware that many organizations take several weeks or longer to respond to inquiries, so allow as much time as possible.

American Enterprise Institute (AEI)
1150 Seventeenth Street NW, Washington, DC   20036
(202) 862-5800 • fax: (202) 862-7177
website: www.aei.org

The nonpartisan American Enterprise Institute (AEI) conducts research and educates both policy makers and the public on issues including the US government, politics, economy, and social welfare. AEI has produced extensive content relating to a variety of wars and conflicts existing in the world, including the war in Afghanistan. Articles covering a range of topics related to Afghanistan can be found on the AEI website and in the magazine of the organization, the *American*.

Amnesty International
5 Penn Plaza, 16th Floor, New York, NY   10001
(212) 807-8400 • fax: (212) 627-1451
website: www.amnestyusa.org

Amnesty International is a global organization consisting of members, activists, and supporters who work on an international scale to combat human rights abuses and protect the rights of all humans as guaranteed by the Universal Declaration of Human Rights and other human rights standards. The organization's website provides analysis of human rights by country, including Afghanistan. "Annual Report: Afghanistan

2013" on the state of human rights in Afghanistan can be read online, along with a blog and numerous articles related to Afghanistan.

Cato Institute
1000 Massachusetts Avenue NW
Washington, DC   20001-5403
(202) 842-0200 • fax: (202) 842-3490
website: www.cato.org

The Cato Institute is a libertarian public policy think tank that espouses the beliefs of individual liberty, limited government, free markets, and peace. In its focus on national security and foreign policy, Cato promotes policy that protects the country but does not engage in empire building or interventionist strategies. Cato experts who write on this topic explore the range of conflict around the globe, including Afghanistan, as well as topics such as terrorism and homeland security. Newsletters, journals, and articles exploring these issues can be read on the Cato website, which also includes the multimedia presentation "The War in Afghanistan: What Went Wrong?"

Center for International Private Enterprise (CIPE)
1155 Fifteenth Street NW, Suite 700, Washington, DC   20005
(202) 721-9200 • (202) 721-9250
e-mail: info@cipe.org
website: www.cipe.org

The Center for International Private Enterprise (CIPE) is an organization that works to strengthen democracy around the world through private enterprise and market-oriented reform. Over the years, CIPE has helped business associations in Afghanistan launch the National Business Agenda (NBA), which contains targeted policy reforms. CIPE has also conducted seminars for numerous Provincial Councils in Afghanistan. Various publications, such as *Democracy in Action* and *OverseasREPORT*, can be found on CIPE's website.

Council on Foreign Relations (CFR)

The Harold Pratt House, 58 East Sixty-Eighth Street
New York, NY 10065
(212) 434-9400 • fax: (212) 434-9800
website: www.cfr.org

The Council on Foreign Relations (CFR) is an independent, nonprofit think tank that focuses on providing analysis and commentary on US foreign policy for government officials, businesspeople, journalists, educators, activists, and civic leaders. CFR features a Studies Program that generates independent research, policy briefs, and analysis. It holds roundtable discussions to bring together experts, senior government officials, journalists, and policy makers to debate topics and generate policy recommendations and solutions to foreign policy issues. CFR publishes *Foreign Affairs*, a magazine on international affairs and foreign policy related to countries throughout the world, including Afghanistan. The organization's website provides a number of articles, analyses, backgrounders, blogs, and expert briefs, as well as an interactive time line detailing the US war in Afghanistan.

Embassy of Afghanistan

2341 Wyoming Avenue NW, Washington, DC 20008
(202) 483-6410 • fax: (202) 483-6488
e-mail: info@embassyofafghanistan.org
website: www.embassyofafghanistan.org

The Embassy of Afghanistan is the diplomatic representation from Afghanistan within the United States. The physical embassy houses the Afghan ambassador and provides a voice for Afghanistan in the United States. The embassy's website offers a monthly newsletter and also provides information about Afghan-American relations as well as general information about Afghanistan. Travel information and required documents for visiting Afghanistan are also available on the website.

Human Rights Watch (HRW)
350 Fifth Avenue, 34th Floor, New York, NY 10118-3299
(212) 290-4700 • fax: (212) 736-1300
website: www.hrw.org

Human Rights Watch (HRW) is an organization that works on the international level to ensure and protect human rights for people worldwide. HRW seeks to ensure that those who commit human rights abuses are held accountable for their actions. Videos, articles, and reports, such as "Afghanistan: Taliban Violence Threatens Election" and "World Report 2014: Afghanistan," can be found on the HRW website.

National Endowment for Democracy (NED)
1025 F Street NW, Suite 800, Washington, DC 20004
(202) 378-9700 • fax: (202) 378-9407
e-mail: info@ned.org
website: www.ned.org

The National Endowment for Democracy (NED) is a private, nonprofit organization that works to develop and strengthen democratic institutions around the world through financial support and other nonviolent methods. NED provides assistance to trade unions, nongovernmental organizations, political parties, independent media, and business organizations struggling to establish democratic institutions and practices in their area. As Afghanistan faced a dysfunctional government and corruption, NED advocated for accountability, improved legislation, and inclusive national policies. NED publishes the *Journal of Democracy* and the *Democracy* e-newsletter, both of which are available on the organization's website.

Peace Action
Montgomery Center, 8630 Fenton Street, Suite 524
Silver Spring, MD 20910
(301) 565-4050 • fax: (301) 565-0850
e-mail: info@peace-action.org
website: www.peace-action.org

Peace Action is a national grassroots peace network that seeks to influence the US Congress and administration through a concerted effort of its national chapters and affiliates. By writing to the government, engaging in Internet and direct actions, and lobbying citizens, the organization attempts to promote peace legislation within the US government. The group's current antiwar issues include ending the war in Afghanistan. Details about the background of this initiative and current actions being taken can be found on Peace Action's website.

United States Department of State
2201 C Street NW, Washington, DC   20520
(202) 647-4000
website: www.state.gov

The United States Department of State is the federal agency that is responsible for formulating, implementing, and assessing US foreign policy. The State Department also assists US citizens living or traveling abroad; promotes and protects US business interests all over the world; and supports the activities of other US federal agencies in foreign countries. The State Department website features a wealth of information on current policies, upcoming events, and updates from various countries, including Afghanistan. It also provides videos, congressional testimony, speech transcripts, background notes, human rights reports, and strategy reviews.

United States Institute of Peace (USIP)
2301 Constitution Avenue NW, Washington, DC   20037
(202) 457-1700 • fax: (202) 429-6063
website: www.usip.org

The United States Institute of Peace (USIP) is an independent conflict-management center tasked by the US Congress with finding peaceful methods to mitigate international conflicts. USIP strives "to save lives, increase the government's ability to deal with conflicts before they escalate, reduce government costs, and enhance our national security." Since 2002, the center has been working to promote peace and stability in Afghanistan. The USIP website offers the publication "Progress in Peacebuilding: Afghanistan," as well as a number of newsletters for the public, including *PeaceBrief, PeaceWatch,* and the *Prevention Newsletter.*

Bibliography of Books

Lina Abirafeh   *Gender and International Aid in
                       Afghanistan: The Politics and Effects of
                       Intervention.* Jefferson, NC:
                       McFarland & Company, 2009.

Anna Badkhen   *Waiting for the Taliban: A Journey
                       Through Northern Afghanistan.* Las
                       Vegas, NV: AmazonEncore, 2010.

Thomas Barfield   *Afghanistan: A Cultural and Political
                       History.* Princeton, NJ: Princeton
                       University Press, 2010.

Kim Barker   *The Taliban Shuffle: Strange Days in
                       Afghanistan and Pakistan.* New York:
                       Anchor Books, 2012.

Shahzad Bashir   *Under the Drones: Modern Lives in
and Robert D.   the Afghanistan-Pakistan Borderlands.*
Crews, eds.   Cambridge, MA: Harvard University
                       Press, 2012.

Rajiv   *Little America: The War Within the
Chandrasekaran   War for Afghanistan.* New York:
                       Vintage Books, 2012.

Noah Coburn   *Derailing Democracy in Afghanistan:
and Anna Larson   Elections in an Unstable Political
                       Landscape.* New York: Columbia
                       University Press, 2013.

John L. Cook   *Afghanistan: The Perfect Failure—A
                       War Doomed by the Coalition's
                       Strategies, Policies and Political
                       Correctness.* Portland, OR: BookBaby,
                       2012.

Theo Farrell, Frans Osinga, and James A. Russell, eds. *Military Adaptation in Afghanistan.* Stanford, CA: Stanford University Press, 2013.

Vanda Felbab-Brown *Aspiration and Ambivalence: Strategies and Realities of Counterinsurgency and State-Building in Afghanistan.* Washington, DC: Brookings Institution Press, 2012.

Paul Fitzgerald and Elizabeth Gould *Invisible History: Afghanistan's Untold Story.* San Francisco, CA: City Lights Publishers, 2009.

Antonio Giustozzi, ed. *Decoding the New Taliban: Insights from the Afghan Field.* New York: Columbia University Press, 2009.

David Isby *Afghanistan: Graveyard of Empires: A New History of the Borderland.* New York: Pegasus Books, 2010.

Seth G. Jones *In the Graveyard of Empires: America's War in Afghanistan.* New York: W.W. Norton & Company, 2010.

David Macdonald *Drugs in Afghanistan: Opium, Outlaws and Scorpion Tales.* Ann Arbor, MI: Pluto Press, 2007.

Carter Malkasian *War Comes to Garmser: Thirty Years of Conflict on the Afghan Frontier.* New York: Oxford University Press, 2013.

Matt J. Martin with Charles W. Sasser	*Predator: The Remote-Control Air War over Iraq and Afghanistan: A Pilot's Story.* Minneapolis, MN: Zenith Press, 2010.
Whit Mason, ed.	*The Rule of Law in Afghanistan: Missing in Inaction.* New York: Cambridge University Press, 2011.
Dipali Mukhopadhyay	*Warlords, Strongman Governors, and the State in Afghanistan.* New York: Cambridge University Press, 2014.
Moska Najib and Nazes Afroz	*Afghanistan—Culture Smart!: The Essential Guide to Customs & Culture.* London: Kuperard, 2013.
Fariba Nawa	*Opium Nation: Child Brides, Drug Lords, and One Woman's Journey Through Afghanistan.* New York: Harper Perennial, 2011.
Ronald E. Neumann	*The Other War: Winning and Losing in Afghanistan.* Dulles, VA: Potomac Books, 2009.
Sean Parnell with John R. Bruning	*Outlaw Platoon: Heroes, Renegades, Infidels, and the Brotherhood of War in Afghanistan.* New York: William Morrow, 2012.
Ahmed Rashid	*Taliban: Militant Islam, Oil and Fundamentalism in Central Asia.* 2nd ed. New Haven, CT: Yale University Press, 2010.

Rosemarie Skaine   *Women of Afghanistan in the Post-Taliban Era: How Lives Have Changed and Where They Stand Today*. Jefferson, NC: McFarland & Company, 2008.

Bing West   *The Wrong War: Grit, Strategy, and the Way Out of Afghanistan*. New York: Random House, 2012.

Brian Glyn Williams   *Afghanistan Declassified: A Guide to America's Longest War*. Philadelphia: University of Pennsylvania Press, 2011.

Index

A

Aaronovitch, David, 203–207
Abdullah, Abdullah, 65–66, 69, 74–80, 83
Adams, Brad, 164
Afghan National Police (ANP)
  corruption, 87, 88, 92, 93, 105–108
  drug addiction, 105, 108
  Taliban preys on corrupt forces, 105–108
  training and pay, 93, 107
  treatment of women, 182
Afghan National Security Forces (ANSF)
  aid, 15, 21, 23–25, 32, 44, 90
  capability, 15, 23
  pay, 107
  responsibility, 15, 21, 23, 68
Afghan Transitional Authority, 49
Afghan Uniform Police (AUP), 106, 107
Afghanistan economy. *See* Economy, Afghanistan
Afghanistan Independent Human Rights Commission (AIHRC), 188
Afghanistan Unveiled (film), 184
Afghanistan War, 2001-, 42*t*
  driven by desire for resources, 113–121
  funding, 20, 21, 23–24, 32, 41, 44, 90–91, 124, 139
  goals, 16, 23, 28, 45, 100, 124, 136

Iran as of central importance, 52–56
not driven by desire for resources, 122–126
settlement, 20–33
US should retain forces, 46–51
US should withdraw completely, 40–45
US soldiers and lives, 22, 32–33, 42*t*
See also Economy, Afghanistan; Media opinion; Public opinion; Withdrawal, of NATO/ISAF from Afghanistan; Withdrawal, of United States from Afghanistan
Agriculture
  food crops, 134–135, 139, 158, 160
  GDP, 127, 130
  new technology, 151
  power, poor nations, 130–131, 132, 140
  transitions away from opium, 127, 139, 140
  transitions to opium, 130–131, 134–135
  transportation challenges, 148
Aid. *See* Foreign aid; Humanitarian aid
AIDS pain medication, 142, 144
Aikins, Matthieu, 18
al-Awlaki, Abdulrahman, 199–200
al-Banna, Ibrahim, 200
al Qaeda
  Afghanistan history, 120–121
  Afghanistan politician connections, 69

O

P